You're Likely *Not* a Racist

Answers for Curious White People

You're Likely *Not* a Racist

Answers for Curious White People

Teresa L. Reed, Ph.D.

GarySprings

Independent Press, LLC
Louisville, Kentucky

You're Likely *Not* a Racist

Published by GarySprings Independent Press, LLC, Louisville, KY.
Edited by Brooklyn Russell, B. Russ Innovations, LLC, Merrillville, IN.
Designed by Terralyn Roach, TSR Creative, Louisville, KY.

ISBN: 978-0-578-95541-4

"Dr. Teresa Reed's book is a gift to White people who want to become educated about racism and race relations in the United States. With patience and compassion, she answers questions that White people are often afraid to ask. She does so by skillfully weaving historical events, current realities, and her experiences as an African American into a narrative that White readers will find compelling. This book is a generous invitation to conversation about race, especially for White Americans who are just beginning to look directly at race."

—Dr. Susan E. Chase, Professor Emeritus of Sociology,
The University of Tulsa

"Dr. Reed has addressed questions and misconceptions about racism and the Black experience in a way that will be illuminating for readers of any race. This book is easy to read, hard to put down, and personally very touching."

—Vernon Howard, Professor Emeritus of Music,
The University of Tulsa

"In this book, often pondered questions, whispered privately, are answered openly against the backdrop of a racially divided nation. *You're Likely Not a Racist* is an olive tree. Its answers are the olive branches for curious readers to extend toward racial equity."

—Kimberly Johnson, Chief Executive Officer,
Tulsa City-County Library

◊

"This is a compelling book for people who really want to understand some of the ways that race, racial difference, and racism have material consequences in the lives of people of African descent in the United States. Dr. Reed answers questions that people may be hesitant to ask, offers accounts from her own experiences, and offers a hopeful way to move forward for people who are genuinely interested in creating an equitable society."

—Dr. Crystal L. Keels, Activist, Author, and Educator

"In *You're Likely Not a Racist: Answers for Curious White People*, Dr. Teresa Reed beautifully weaves together current events, social commentary, history, and her personal story in a way that adds a unique perspective to the conversation about race in the United States.

Speaking directly to White Americans, Dr. Reed builds on her experience with "Safe Saturdays" at the University of Louisville to create a casual and comfortable space for White people to understand and appreciate the uncomfortable truths of racism and the Black experience. As she describes it, Dr. Reed addresses the reader "casually as [her] friend, as though... having coffee at Starbucks . . . .". The tone is inviting and warm, without ever shying away from painful realities, in a way that allows the reader to listen to understand instead of listening to respond and makes the book hard to put down."

— David Miller, Director of Educational Initiatives,
Director of the Center for Service and Global Citizenship,
Deerfield Academy

DEDICATION

I dedicate this book to the memory of my mother

Tobi Lorraine Upshaw Shelton
(1942–2020)

whose compassion was unparalleled and whose
love for humanity knew no bounds.

I honor the memory of our ancestors

Jessie Lee Mahone Parkman
(1900–1980)

and

John Walker Parkman
(1876–1950)

whose forbidden love I proudly bring
into the light of this more intelligent
and hopeful day.

Compassion compels me to write this book. Compassion moves me to speak directly to White people who wish to move toward a fuller, more authentic understanding of African Americans and people of color in general. In these pages, I answer, without judgement, several of the important, honest questions that many White people have about race but are afraid to ask.

CONTENTS

Introduction..xi

What This Book is Not; What This Book Is.............................xix

1. My Introduction to Whiteness...1

2. Obvious and Invisible..9

3. The Dangerous Bliss of White Ignorance.........................15

Answers to Questions White People May Be Afraid to Ask.........23

4. Let the Conversation Begin: Our Rules of Engagement.............25

5. Why Do Black People Seem
   to Think About Race All of the Time?...........................29

6. Why Do Black People Seem So Angry?............................33

7. Why Do Black People Seem to Want Special Favors?.................43

8. Why Can't Black People Pull Themselves
   Up by Their Bootstraps Like My Ancestors Did?.......................49

9. Why Do Black Neighborhoods Often
   Seem Dirty, Run Down, and Dangerous?.......................61

10. Am I a Racist if I Prefer to Be With My Own Kind?.................67

11. Am I a Racist for Wanting to Keep
    Crime Out of My Safe and Peaceful Community?.......................73

12. Why Do Black People Get Away With
    Saying the "N" Word When White People Cannot?.................85

13. Why Do Black People Continue to Complain
    Even After the Election of Barack Obama?......97

14. Why Do I Feel Threatened by Successful Black People?......105

15. Am I a Racist if I Don't Want My Taxes to
    Provide Welfare for People Who Won't Work?......113

16. Isn't Affirmative Action Racist
    Because It Gives Preference Based Upon Race?......119

17. Why Don't Black People Accept and
    Welcome Me When I Try to Interact With Them?......125

18. Why Can't Black People Forget About
    Slavery, Let Go of the Past, and Move On?......129

19. Why Is There So Much Attention to Black Lives Matter?......137

20. As a White American, How Can I
    Respond Effectively to Racial Injustice?......151

Let the Healing Begin......165

21. We Are Family
    (Dysfunctional Perhaps, but Family Nonetheless)......167

Appendix: My June 2020 letter to the
University of Louisville School of Music......188

Acknowledgments......201

Notes......203

Index......215

INTRODUCTION

Spring 2020 was tumultuous. In early March, my dear friend sped home to Michigan to be at his dying father's side. A minister in otherwise good health, his father had fallen ill with pneumonia, which showed no signs of abating. Within days, nearly 30 of his colleagues, also ministers, had similar, pneumonia-like symptoms. Within weeks, my friend's father and more than two dozen of those colleagues would be dead from the Coronavirus.

COVID-19 was mysterious, fierce, contagious, and becoming a daily headline. Before the end of March, many schools and businesses were either closed or migrating to remote operation. I head the School of Music at the University of Louisville. Our university leadership called an emergency meeting just before the end of Spring Break, announcing that our students would remain away from campus and would finish the semester online.

As we grappled with fears and uncertainties related to COVID-19, our city took center stage in an escalating national drama of racial unrest. Tensions between communities of color and the American justice system were generations old; in Spring 2020, those tensions seemed to reach fever pitch.

The roots of the tension ran deep. Eight years prior, in February 2012, 17-year-old Trayvon Martin was returning from a Sanford, Florida 7-Eleven to the home of his father's fiance' where the two were visiting that evening. As he walked back to the home with the Skittles and tea he'd purchased,

Martin was followed and accosted. Within minutes, he was killed by neighborhood watch captain George Zimmerman. Martin was unarmed. Zimmerman was both armed and the aggressor. Martin's killing, and the subsequent acquittal of Zimmerman in July 2013, sparked nationwide protests. Zimmerman (whose mother was born in Peru and whose father is a White man) expressed no remorse. He auctioned the murder weapon on eBay, which is believed to have sold for over $100,000.[1]

Stories parallel to Martin's—accounts of unarmed African American people who were swiftly killed by White people who deemed them to be "suspicious"—proliferated in the years that followed. Spring 2020 was particularly deadly for Black people going about the routine activities of their daily lives. On February 23, 2020, Ahmaud Arbery was killed while jogging in his Glynn County, Georgia neighborhood. On March 13, Breonna Taylor was killed in my city, Louisville, Kentucky, as she slept in her apartment. On May 25, George Floyd was suffocated to death (as the camera rolled) by a Minneapolis officer who leaned on his neck for 9 minutes and 29 seconds. Arbery, Taylor, and Floyd were unarmed, and none of the three had been proven guilty of any crime. Nonetheless, all three, like Trayvon Martin, were summarily erased from the families and communities that loved them.

In Louisville, tensions around Breonna Taylor's death were at the boiling point. Nightly protests filled the streets—the crowds increasing in numbers as calls for justice seemed to go unheard. In June, University of Louisville President Neeli Bendapudi issued a statement acknowledging the pain in our community and affirming U of L's commitment to diversity, equity, inclusion, and justice. She called upon each of the deans to address statements to their own academic units.

As I began to draft my message to the School of Music, I had to reckon with my own lingering pain from yet another such tragedy, one that hit dreadfully close to home. In 2016, when I lived in Tulsa, Oklahoma, a long-time friend of mine lost his son under circumstances very similar to those surrounding the deaths of Arbery, Taylor, and Floyd. On the evening of September 16th of that year, Terence Crutcher's car was stalled in the middle of the street in a North Tulsa neighborhood. Police were called and arrived at the scene. Before Terence could get assistance, Officer Betty Shelby discharged her weapon, shooting Terence in the back, killing him as his hands were raised in surrender. He was unarmed. After the city erupted in protests, Shelby was arrested. The following year, on May 17, 2017, she was found not guilty. She got a new job as a gun instructor for the National Rifle Association.[2]

To this day, I have in my iPhone the widely disseminated police dashcam photograph of Terence Crutcher with his hands raised moments before he was killed. Answering President Bendapudi's request, I put pen to paper and began to draft my message to the School of Music (that letter is reproduced in the Appendix). What spilled forth was my own unprocessed trauma. I was surprised by the immediacy of the grief that still lived inside of my own soul, a personal, piercing grief to which I confessed in the message that I wrote and disseminated to the School of Music.

Alongside my expression of pain and outrage, however, I offered hope. Perhaps it was an irrational hope. Yet, it was—and remains—a powerful and stubborn hope grounded in my belief that in every human being, there is a kernel of goodness. However distorted, concealed, diminished, misguided, or camouflaged it may be, I believe the kernel of goodness is there.

I have yet to heal fully from the tragic loss of Terence Crutcher, and I continue to grieve for Trayvon Martin, Ahmaud Arbery, Breonna Taylor, George Floyd, and for so many others killed simply because someone perceived them to be suspicious or dangerous. Their names are too numerous to list here.

But my healing has begun. What started my healing was not the protests, marches, or the sharing of pain with others who felt my same trauma; instead, my healing started at the moment when I discovered that the power of friendship was stronger than the offense of White racism. In my pain, I reached out to a long-time White friend, and she was brave enough to see me fully in the context of what it means to be a Black person in America.

After the arrest of Betty Shelby, the city of Tulsa held its breath for months, waiting for the outcome of the trial, hopeful that there would be justice for Terence Crutcher. The Crutchers were known in the city for their musical talent, and they were well loved in the Black community. Terence's father, Reverend Joey Crutcher, was a long-time friend and had been the musician at my wedding some 20 years earlier. The police dashcam had captured the incident. By the time of Shelby's trial, millions of people around the country had already seen the footage of Terence with his hands in the air and his back to the officers moments before he was senselessly gunned down. The evidence could not have been more compelling. Terence did not appear to pose any threat whatsoever. Had he posed a threat, he could have been handcuffed; he could have been tazed. But he did not have to die.

When the verdict was returned on May 17, 2017, the Black community of Tulsa was in shock and disbelief. At the same time, many White people expressed relief that Terence had gotten what he deserved, and they congratulated Shelby for her valor and quick thinking. It felt as though there was an irreconcilable chasm between these two perspectives. While Black people grieved, many White people celebrated. The news coverage was biased, painting Terence as a villain with a drug problem, while painting Shelby as a hero who had done a great job. I was in desperate need of a reason to refrain from hating everyone and everything that failed Terence Crutcher.

Still reeling in shock that day following the announcement of Betty Shelby's acquittal, I took out my phone and I sent a text to my friend, my White friend that I had known for some 20 years. Until that moment, we had talked about many things, but never about race. I didn't know what her reaction would be. But on the afternoon of May 17, I took a chance. My text message to her was simple: "I am not well."

She understood. She was a White person—as White as the officer who pulled the trigger—yet, *she got it.* Her loving, compassionate, and empathetic response was what I needed in that moment. She was the reason that I chose hope over hatred.

In my written statement to the School of Music, I shared my healing encounter with my White friend. To my surprise, my statement was widely circulated. The feedback from my campus community—many of them White colleagues and students—was rapid and overwhelming. There were scores of White people who felt pain at seeing how fractured our community and our world had become. They struggled to understand, and they wanted to learn more.

To answer their curiosity and concern, I began to host a weekly series of candid conversations about race every Saturday morning at 9am on a Zoom call. Coined "Safe

Saturday Conversations about Race," my objective was to create a nonthreatening forum where White people and African American people could share their perspectives, learn from one another, and engage in a judgement-free, healing dialogue. In those conversations, White people were invited to wonder out loud about everything, from interracial relationships to religion and racism, to use of the "N" word. No topic was taboo; nothing was off-limits. They got to voice their questions without fear of backlash; and Black people answered, sharing their stories with candor, teaching their White colleagues, and honoring their curiosity with information.

It is in the spirit of "Safe Saturdays" that I offer this book. I am confident that racism can be conquered if we are brave and determined enough to get at the ignorance that feeds it.

What this Book Is Not; What this Book Is

This book is not a textbook, nor is it an academic or philosophical treatise. It makes no attempt to explore, respond to, or critique existing theories of race. There are many wonderful scholars and excellent books devoted to that work, which is worthwhile and extremely important. Although I've included research, this book is not offered as rigorous scholarship. Although I discuss history, I do not offer this as a history book. This book, instead, is a conversation that blends memoire and historical evidence with the goal of developing trust and friendship with the reader.

In the title of this book, I contend that you are likely *not* a racist. Here are some simple working definitions. The term *racist* can be both a noun, referring to a type of person, and an adjective used to describe something (e.g., *racist policies, racist systems, a racist joke*). For our purposes, I'll define *racist* as a person who has resolved that a human being's worth is based upon the color of their skin, and whose normal, consistent behavior and treatment of others reflects this belief. For example, a racist is persuaded that White people are inherently superior by virtue of their Whiteness, and that people of color are inherently inferior because they are not White.[3]

Racist policies, racist systems, and racist jokes are ones that align with the notion that a human being's worth is based upon their skin color or race. When racists use their power to act upon this belief, they can feel justified in oppressing people that they consider to be racially inferior.

I would argue that most White Americans are not racists. However, too many are profoundly undereducated and uninformed. They go through life harboring legitimate questions about race that they simply don't ask for fear of using the wrong words, or of triggering an uncomfortable reaction, or of being called a racist.

The silent questions are sometimes those most in need of answers. In the pages that follow, there is safety—safety to wonder, to ask, to learn, and to grow. And from this safe place, we can all begin to heal together. If you are holding this book and reading these words with a curious mind and an open heart, you are likely not a racist. Instead, you may be hungry for knowledge, thirsty for change, and ready for both.

1

My
Introduction
to
Whiteness

In September 1969, I started at Ivanhoe Elementary School in Gary, Indiana. Mrs. Lasser was my kindergarten teacher. She was slender, tall, and wore pastel dresses, wire-framed glasses, and tan orthopedic shoes. She seemed to tip-toe when she walked, and she rarely spoke above a whisper. She kept a peaceful and disciplined classroom. She had us form a line two abreast whenever we went for restroom breaks or to gym, art, or music. She always held the hand of the student on the left at the front of the line, and I distinctly remember the way my hand felt inside of hers. Her grip was gentle and warm, and her skin was thin and wrinkled like delicate, threadbare silk. I felt safe in her class because days there were orderly and predictable, and she always nurtured and affirmed us—celebrating our genius with every properly traced letter or creative rendering of construction paper, Popsicle sticks, and glue. Every Friday afternoon, she rewarded each of us for a week's work with exactly two cookies atop a square paper napkin. All of the kids in my kindergarten class were children of color. Mrs. Lasser was a White woman.

After school, I'd settle in with my half of a bologna sandwich to watch *Romper Room*. An afternoon kids' television show, *Romper Room* always ended with the hostess peering through a magic mirror that showed her the faces of her young viewing audience. She'd then call the names of those she could see: "I see Susan, and Mary, and Steven, and

John; I see Sallie, and Benjamin, and Martha, and Craig . . .". As for perhaps millions of children, the daily draw to *Romper Room* was the hope that I might be seen through the magic mirror and that she would call my name, or perhaps the name of someone I knew. There was never anyone that looked like me on *Romper Room*, yet, I imagined that her magic mirror allowed her to see that I was there.

Fast-forward to 1983, when I left my home in Gary for college. On a steamy Saturday morning in August, we loaded my modest belongings into our white Station Wagon bound for Valparaiso University. As we headed east on US Highway 30, my mom, dad, and I, each in our own thoughts, reflected upon the bittersweetness of endings and beginnings and the lure of new horizons. My dad lowered his driver's side car window and lit a cigarette, always an indication that he was deep in thought. He then turned on the radio to fill the silence. We welcomed the distraction from the clear discomfort of that moment, a strange mixture of excitement and fear of the unknown. My dad turned the knob to adjust the volume. Breaking news reported that tennis star Billie Jean King, who shortly before had come out as a lesbian, was retiring from professional sports. That story was the soundtrack of my transition from life in Gary to a new and unfamiliar world.

Finally, we exited US Highway 30 onto the open greenspace with its collection of collegiate buildings, some of them hallowed halls covered in ivy, others more modern. An imposing chapel with a towering stained-glass front stood as the centerpiece of the landscape. We followed the signage through the campus, passing Mueller Hall and Dickmeyer Hall on the way to my new home, Kreinheder Hall. It struck me in that moment that those were all German names. German names were rare in Gary.

We parked in front of the dorm and carted my two suitcases, footlocker, laundry basket, and saxophone up the three flights of stairs to Room 338. With the last of my things unloaded, my parents gave me words of wisdom, an envelope with $200 for pocket change, and a parting embrace with instructions to call as often as I needed. Although it had only taken us 45 minutes to drive there, we knew immediately that we were far from home. Leaving me standing on the sidewalk in front of the dorm, they departed, the white Station Wagon shrinking from my view as they drove farther into the distance to head now westbound on US 30. A lump formed in my throat, and I fought back salty, stubborn tears, instantly missing my parents and four sisters, but cautiously intrigued by my new surroundings.

I spent my first days on campus in Freshman Orientation, which was both an over-the-top welcome and a crash-course in all things "Valpo." The itinerary for orientation week was so packed that, at first, there was little time for homesickness. But I'd soon find that I'd left the comfort and safety of my affirming, majority-Black community for what was essentially a foreign country. I was in the extreme minority. Although less than an hour away, Valparaiso University was a vast departure from what I'd always known.

In general, people were polite; many were friendly. Yet, I was one of seven African American students in Valparaiso's Fall 1983 entering freshman class, and one of 27 persons of African descent on the campus of roughly 5,000. I was one of three African American women in Kreinheder Hall, one of three African American students in the Department of Music, and the lone African American student in most of the classes I'd take there for the next four years. I studied with no professors of color in my undergraduate courses. My entire undergraduate music curriculum covered no Black artists or composers, and no historical figures of color. In the early 1980s, *diversity* was on no one's radar; the word had not yet become part of anyone's vocabulary of social consciousness. Those of us who were African American swiftly found and clung to each other knowing that we were guests who had received a lukewarm welcome into *their* world. At that time, no one considered Valparaiso's racial makeup to be in need of correction.

While my White peers seemed to acclimate to Valpo with ease, I experienced culture shock. Many of the comforts of Gary that I'd taken for granted were gone. There were no stores in the city of Valparaiso that carried pantyhose or makeup that matched my skin tone. The products I needed to care for my "ethnic" hair were nowhere to be found. There were no copies of *Ebony* or *Jet* magazines on any store or library shelf. The R&B and Black gospel music that I loved were nonexistent, except on my own battery-operated Walkman and the few cassette tapes that I owned. Instead, the air was filled with Bonnie Tyler's "Total Eclipse of the Heart," the Eurythmics' "Sweet Dreams," and Elton John's "I Guess That's Why They Call it the Blues." The spirit and energy of my Black Pentecostal upbringing were millions of miles away from Valparaiso, where, instead, religion was measured, controlled, and went perfectly according to script. Many of the familiar foods of my hometown were unknown in Valparaiso. Instead, I learned about bagels, brats, and sushi, and I saw people drink tomato juice for breakfast and put ketchup on eggs for the first time in my life. I also learned that complete strangers who knew nothing about me had definite, pre-formed opinions about who I was.

For me, college quickly became about both education and survival. In order to survive both mentally and socially, I had to embark upon an accelerated, self-guided study of Whiteness. Of course, popular culture had exposed me to Whiteness my entire life, and there were some predominantly White towns adjacent to Gary. Mrs. Lasser, my kindergarten teacher, was a White person, and so was Mr. Hubbard, my elementary school principal. Yet, Mrs. Lasser and Mr.

Hubbard occupied a special category of Whiteness in our world, where they functioned in positions of authority and leadership while among us but then departed Gary for their racial/social comfort zones once the workday ended.

Until college, I was largely detached from any day-to-day reality where I was completely immersed in a White world. The college experience made me realize how incredibly sheltered I had been. Life in Gary was familiar, comfortable, self-contained, and affirming—a Black oasis that existed apart from the broader, non-Black reality. But living in Valparaiso erased the safety and comfort of that detachment. It placed me in a sometimes-hostile environment where the contrast between my skin and theirs framed my entire way of being in that space for four very long years.

2

Obvious
and
Invisible

Throughout my undergraduate years, Valparaiso's mascot was the Crusader. A thoroughly Lutheran university, Valpo took great pride in its Christian, Protestant heritage. Symbols, lessons, and references to Martin Luther and the Reformation were woven throughout Valpo culture. And in this culture, the symbol of the Crusader was normalized and revered. No one ever mentioned, acknowledged, or seemed to mind that Crusaders were militant European Christians who exacted violence against people of color in the name of God (it was just in January 2021 that the University decided to retire this mascot).[1]

Throughout undergrad, my Blackness made me both very obvious and very invisible. My brown skin always announced and underscored my presence. Whenever I took a shower, for example, my brown legs and feet gave away my identity, robbing me of the anonymity that one might expect when attending to private business. As the only Black student in almost all of my classes, I became the *de facto* spokesperson for my entire race. It was suddenly my responsibility to critique my every word and action as having the potential to reflect positively or negatively upon us all.

I became obvious in other ways that I didn't expect. As a freshman music major and a wind player, I was enrolled in the Crusader Marching Band. Anyone who's ever been in a marching band knows that it's both great fun and grueling work. Thanks to a shared love for music, together with hours of practice in less-than-great conditions, marching band students develop a special bond. I found a home there among friends, many of them music majors like me. One of our big performances was in the Popcorn Festival that the city of Valparaiso held annually, Orville Redenbacher being one of Valpo's native sons. In our brown and yellow polyester Crusader uniforms, we marched in formation through the city's main street playing the Sousa piece we'd rehearsed for the occasion. I was focused on the music, making sure to keep in step with my shoulders exactly in line with those to the right and left of me. It felt good to have found my fit and to feel a sense of comradery with my bandmates.

And then, from the sidelines, one of the townspeople yelled out, "Hey, look at the nigger!" Until that moment, I'd forgotten that I was the only Black student in the band. Upon hearing those words, however, I was jarred into an unpleasant awareness. My insides cringed. I looked straight ahead. I kept marching, kept playing, showing no reaction. I pretended that I hadn't heard.

And then there was the time that I walked into my 9:00 a.m. theory class to find that a classmate had drawn a caricature of me on the board. The figure he drew was grotesque but unmistakable. He wasn't a very good artist. To clarify his intent, he labeled his depiction "BLACK PERSON." He thought it was funny, as did several of my classmates. I was the only Black person in the class, and at that time, one of just two African American students in the entire Music Department. I always sat on the front row, so the drawing was directly in front of me. I pretended not to notice, although the air was thick with expectation for me to react. His artwork remained on the board until my professor erased it to illustrate something about figured bass realization.

And so passed for me the months and years that followed. I took my classes, wrote papers, studied for exams, and buried myself in my music. Along the way, I found some friendships and mentors, dated, fell in and out of love, heard insults, became the subject of ridicule, and felt at once afraid, inspired, and determined. During peaceful times, I could be startled into remembering that, to many, my very appearance was offensive. I kept marching, filtering my reactions, finding safety where I could, and focusing on the attainment of my degree.

Although the distinction of my skin made me obvious, there were times when my Blackness made me invisible. My most enduring memory of graduation day from Valparaiso University was the processional at the start of the commencement ceremony. The Class of 1987 was gathered outside of the gymnasium, and I was with the subset of chatty and excited music majors waiting for the proceedings to begin. Dressed in identical caps and gowns, I felt a part of this proud group of soon-to-be Valpo alumni. Like the band uniform that had afforded me a sense of belonging, the regalia I wore that day provided a way for me to blend in.

And then the marshal announced that the processional was ready to begin. Through his bullhorn, he instructed us to form ourselves into a line, with rows four abreast. The conversation dissipated as the graduates heeded the marshal's instructions, each one of us scrambling to link ourselves in formation with three others. To no avail, I tried to place myself in a row of four across, but each row I joined instantly reconfigured, excluding me. The band had begun to play *Pomp and Circumstance.* The line of graduates began the grand forward march. There I was, the lone African American graduate for as far as my eye could see, walking as a row of one until an usher noticed and inserted me elsewhere in the line. If only Mrs. Lasser had been there to hold my hand . . . .

In my mind's eye, I had imagined that graduation day would conclude with celebratory, perhaps even tearful goodbye embraces with those classmates alongside whom I had worked, studied, practiced, and performed since Fall 1983. Valpo had its tough moments for me. But there were also rich and rewarding moments and people that I wanted to remember. There were those to whom I wanted to say, "Goodbye and good luck. Let's keep in touch. Here's where you can reach me."

But the kind of closure I imagined never happened. Once the commencement ceremony had ended, my classmates all scattered, each one joining their families and preferred social circles. White peers who had been my classmates for four years, and who I considered to be my friends, looked away that day. They made no eye contact with me in the presence of their loved ones who might notice.

But I was not alone. The affirmation from my family and from a few of my professors that day helped me to choose celebration over disappointment. Still, decades later, being both obvious and invisible at Valparaiso University sticks painfully with me, and graduation day was an accurate summary of that undergraduate experience.

3

The Dangerous Bliss
of
White Ignorance

Surviving in the White world of Valparaiso University, in the early 1980s, meant that I had to learn how White people thought; I had to understand what they valued, what they feared, and why. I had to learn their history, their triggers, their motivations, and the boundaries of their comfort zones. I had to learn which parts of my Black identity I could safely expose, which parts were best to conceal, which parts of my perspective to voice, and which parts to mute. And I had to learn this, not through books or from a distance, but by interacting with them on a daily basis, having conversations with them, working alongside them, and engaging with them in common experiences. And I had to learn the lessons of Whiteness well enough to become a functional citizen of their world, to interact amicably with others, and to persist through to the completion of my study.

That was over 30 years ago. Since the days of my crash course in Whiteness at Valparaiso University, I've had the great blessing of a long, fruitful, and rewarding career in academia. I've enjoyed meaningful interactions and friendships with people from every racial and ethnic background—many representing nationalities and cultures from around the world. I am radically inclusive in my thinking and in my spiritual and ethical conviction, and I honor and value all human beings, whatever their racial, ethnic, national, political, religious, or gender identities. Compassion is the cornerstone of my religion. I strongly identify with those who are marked and isolated by difference. I know what it's like to be the subject of unsavory narratives about the *other*, narratives that I work to prevent taking root in my own mind.

Fast-forward to the racial turbulence of the present day. In 2021, America is dangerously polarized. No one who is attuned to reality can turn fully away from stories that most clearly underscore the ills of our society. There is both a need to address the issue of race/racism and, too often, complete confusion about where to begin. Race and racism have taken center stage in our current events, but many with even the best of intentions find themselves at a loss for how to engage the conversations that can bring genuine understanding.

Too many White Americans—particularly those in my age group—are disturbed by the racial unrest that has become all too common; yet, they have no understanding of its source. They have only a shallow and often misguided knowledge of African American people. They are largely ignorant about what Black people think, what Black people value, what we fear, what incentivizes us, and why. They know almost nothing of our history, our triggers, our motivations, what affirms us or what threatens us. They see outcries, demands, and protests, but have no real understanding of what sparked these tensions in the first place.

Most White Americans will live their entire lives and never experience being in the racial minority. Even those White people who are otherwise marginalized, by gender or by national origin, for example, will never see life from the lens of someone whose skin marks them as different. There was zero incentive for any of my White peers at Valparaiso University to educate themselves on Blackness. Learning about people of color—particularly for White Americans who entered adulthood in the pre-digital age—was 100% optional. For White Americans, navigating safely, productively, and prosperously through life generally requires intimate knowledge of no racial group except their own.

The result is millions upon millions of White people who, today, share this country with an ever-growing population of people of color who they simply don't understand. This lack of understanding has been a generations-old breeding ground for fear, the kind of fear that sees a threat in brown skin even when no actual threat exists.

The presidential elections of 2016 and 2020 provide strong evidence of this fact. White supremacist groups, including the Proud Boys, the KKK, and the Neo-Nazis, are outspoken and enthusiastic in their support for twice-impeached former President Donald Trump. Trump remains for these hate groups a powerful symbol of White supremacy and a champion of their values. Said another way, while Trump has claimed to not be a racist (in his words, "the least racist person you'll ever meet"), White supremacist groups recognize and proudly claim him as one of their own.[1] While members of overtly white supremacist groups may be a minority, nearly 62 million Americans voted for Trump in 2016, and 74 million voted for him in 2020. This means that well into the 21st century, as many as 74 million Americans either 1) don't understand what racism is, 2) don't recognize that Trump is a racist, or 3) they recognize that he is a racist but are unbothered by this fact or are not bothered by it enough to have voted for someone else.[2]

The 2020 presidential campaign concluded with the election of Joseph Biden as President and Kamala Harris as Vice President. Joe Biden had served as Vice President alongside the first African American president, Barack Obama. Kamala Harris made history as the first female and the first Black Vice-President, the daughter of Indian and Jamaican immigrants. Many Americans celebrated these milestones. And many others did not.

On January 6, 2021, thousands of Americans— overwhelmingly White—descended upon Washington D.C. at the invitation of President Trump. They had come, not only to protest the election results, but to overturn those election results by violent force.

Among them were blatant symbols of racism, including a noose and gallows, suggestive of death by hanging, and a guillotine, suggestive of beheading; the "OK" symbol of White power, the Confederate flag, and nostalgic references to Auschwitz, including the chilling acronym "6MWE" (Six

Million Wasn't Enough) emblazoned on T-shirts and baseball caps. Along with these symbols and images were numerous red MAGA ("Make America Great Again") caps and many giant TRUMP flags. The angry mob stormed the United States Capitol, scaling its walls, shattering windows, and vandalizing its interior. They succeeded in interrupting the official electoral count for several hours. Capitol police were overwhelmed by the mob of insurrectionists and were unable to contain the chaos. Shots were fired. Blood was shed. Five died. Guns were drawn, glass was shattered, and police officers were beaten. A curfew was imposed but ignored, and for hours, there were no arrests.

I am confident that the overwhelming majority of White people are well-intentioned and good-hearted. In fact, many of those who stormed the Capitol on January 6 were everyday Americans and otherwise upstanding citizens—teachers, housewives, accountants, construction workers, ministers—who were radicalized by a message of fear and hatred rooted deeply in the crippling ignorance about race from which too many White people suffer.

Due to the gaps in their knowledge and the shallowness of their experience, many otherwise good White folks are at a genuine loss when it comes to understanding race and racism. (This may be especially true of White people who came of age before multicultural trends in education and before the Digital Age afforded nearly boundless opportunities for social awareness.) They've never been afforded any exposure to people of color that parallels my own White immersion experience at Valparaiso University. Consequently, too many White Americans suffer not from an intrinsically hateful disposition, but from profound and utter ignorance. It is this ignorance that feeds racism, turning otherwise peace-loving White Americans into purveyors of the criminal acts that the world witnessed at the U.S. Capitol on January 6.

No sane person wishes to live in a state of destructive ignorance. I would argue further that no one wishes to be racist, as even racists themselves often deny that they are. We all suffer from the limitations of our backgrounds and upbringings. And we are all vulnerable to biases of different sorts. For each one of us, reality includes some truths but excludes others. We are all blinded in some sense, some of us by our history of oppression, some of us by our history of privilege. We cannot know what we have never been taught; we cannot understand what we have never had opportunity to learn. There is but one remedy, one correction for ignorance: education.

And so, compassion compels me to speak directly to White people who wish to move in the direction of a fuller, more authentic understanding of African Americans and people of color in general. In the pages that follow, I answer, without judgement, several of the important, honest questions that many White people have about race but are afraid to ask.

Please note: I make no claim to be the representative voice for all Black people. African American people are quite diverse in thought, background, socio-economic status, national origin, and religious and political preference. While there is no way that I can articulate what all Black people think and feel, I do believe that I can share information of value about some very typical aspects of the Black experience in America. I also believe that I can help to facilitate a safe, inclusive, informative, and affirming discourse about race that has been long overdue.

The answers I give are to questions that White people may hesitate to ask for fear that they are too awkward, delicate, sensitive, and/or potentially offensive. By addressing these questions with objectivity and candor, it is my hope that information and clarity can dispel ignorance and fear, and that the racial tensions that so plague our times will begin to dissipate. In their place, I hope for the emergence of a new trend of authentic friendships across racial differences; and I imagine a day when these differences are no longer feared or merely tolerated but are heartily celebrated.

Answers to Questions

White People May

Be Afraid to Ask

4

Let the Conversation Begin:
Our Rules of Engagement

A few years ago, a colleague came to me late in the spring semester distraught about a student in one of her courses. This young woman, a freshman, was struggling to adapt to the norms and standards of college life. She was bright, articulate, talented, and quite capable of succeeding. She was also chronically absent from class, delinquent on assignments, and had failed to sit for several exams. Despite her academic problems, she remained highly visible around campus. She was an enthusiastic participant in extracurricular activities and a leader in student organizations. By late April, it was apparent that she had crossed the point of no return and was certain to fail the course. In early May, however, within days of the semester's end, she approached my colleague seeking mercy and an 11th-hour pathway for redemption. When my colleague refused, the student became incensed and accused her of being a racist. My colleague was a White woman; the student in question was an African American woman.

My colleague's syllabus clearly detailed the requirements of her class, none of which the young woman had fulfilled. Despite the fact that this student had earned her failure, my colleague sought from me reassurance that she was, in fact, not a racist. I put her fears to rest. I explained to her the difference between students who were genuine victims of systematic educational inequities, and students who were simply immature and not yet disciplined enough for the rigors of college life. I then pointed out that this same student was also failing one of my courses and had made a similar last-minute appeal to me, which I also denied. That conversation led to a broader and richer discussion about race and racism, one that left my colleague enlightened and reassured and our friendship enhanced and strengthened.

In the chapters that follow, I am speaking directly to White Americans. When I use the word *you*, I am speaking directly to the reader, who I presume to be White. I am addressing you casually as my friend, as though the two of us are having coffee at Starbucks. When I use the plural *you*, I imagine myself addressing a group of White friends or listeners, or White people in general, and the setting is as amicable and nonthreatening as cocktail-hour conversation.

When I use the term *we*, I am speaking of African American people, myself included. Please note, however, that I am offering my own perspective. I've lived in both the predominantly Black world of my Gary, Indiana upbringing and in the predominantly White world of higher education for about the past thirty years. Over the course of my career, I've taught students numbering in the thousands, students from around the United States and the world. I believe that I'm amply qualified to give voice to some of the most typical experiences of Black people in this country. I respect, however, that there are Black people who may have points of view that are very different than mine.

I will use the terms *Black, Black American,* and *African American* interchangeably. I will sometimes refer to *people of color,* which means both African American people and other non-White populations.

I will use the terms *White people* and *White Americans* to reference this country's dominant racial category.

Each chapter that follows is a question followed by an answer. The questions are ones that I've heard White people ask over the years in various settings (in meetings, in classes, over the media, around the water cooler . . . .). These are questions that I've read, that I've heard asked to others, and in some cases, questions that have been posed directly to me.

Each answer is formatted in two sections: A *Short Answer,* followed by a more extensive section titled *More to Consider.* Along the way, I will share some of my own experiences to help illustrate certain points.

By design, our conversation is an uneven exchange, as I am doing all of the talking and you are doing the listening. Your listening, however, is radically brave and courageous; your reflection on the information I share has the potential to fill gaps in your knowledge about race in ways that are personally transformative for you, and ultimately impactful for the good of our society.

5

Why Do Black People Seem to Think About Race All of the Time?

The Short Answer

Black people think about race and racism only to the extent that they are impacted by race and racism. African American people are often judged, assessed, regarded, and treated in accordance with the way others feel about the color of their darker skin. We think about race and racism because society reminds us to do so on a fairly regular basis.

More to Consider

Reminders about race and racism are a constant reality for many people of color. When I was a student at Valparaiso, I was reminded quite frequently that I was different, something that I usually forgot about until some experience jarred me into remembering.

Thinking about race is not always a negative thing, however. I love being an African American woman. I love my brown skin, my thicker lips, and my tightly coiled hair. I love the customs and the food of my heritage, and I don't mind that my weight sometimes fluctuates to reflect this fact. I celebrate my culture, and I am inspired by the history of my people. I marvel at the remarkable, odds-defying achievements of my ancestors and of Black people in general. Ours is a beautiful story—the positive aspects of which are not told often enough.

Sometimes, reminders about race and racial difference have come in the form of invitations to offer, in various contexts, my perspective as an African American person.

Years after I graduated from Valparaiso, I was invited back as an alumna to lecture on African American music. The first course I was invited to teach at the University of Tulsa was "Black American Musical Experience," and I also taught courses in Black gospel music, Black composers of classical music, and rhythm & blues.

Although my Ph.D. is in Music Theory with doctoral minors in Music History and Literature and African American Studies, I have been called upon to speak and write about issues of race and racial difference in public settings much more frequently than I have been asked to address 16th-century counterpoint or pitch class sets. For about the past 30 years, invitations to discuss race and racial difference at community events, churches, and in a variety of professional and academic settings have been constant. I continue to serve on multiple panels and committees related to diversity, equity, inclusion, and antiracism in large part because I am an African American person. And my experience is far from unique. Black professionals, regardless of their specializations, often find themselves answering the call to explain or address matters of race and racial difference in the absence of others who can offer the perspective that comes with the lived experience of being in the minority.

Although race is one dimension of my identity, no one asks my perspective as a woman, or as an Indiana native, or as a daughter, wife, sister, aunt, author, teacher, musician, or animal lover. Race is often perceived to be the most salient characteristic about people of color.

6

Why Do Black People
Seem So Angry?

The Short Answer

L ike all others, African American people experience the full range of human emotions—love, compassion, joy, grief, and, of course, anger. If your primary exposure to Black people is through what you view on television, learn on the news, see online, or read in the paper, you may get the impression that Black people are angry most of the time. While this is certainly not the case, in the absence of any other knowledge, this perception is understandable.

More to Consider

In 1999, David Howard was the Director of Constituent Services for the mayor of Washington, D.C.. Howard, who was a White man, was actively and visibly supportive of then-mayor Anthony Williams, who was a Black man. A graduate of the University of Florida with a degree in Economics, Howard, by all accounts, was a kind person and a good citizen. He was the coordinator of the 1,600 volunteers who worked to get Williams elected, and then took a job with the city overseeing the office charged with responding to a variety of citizen complaints. And then, on January 15, 1999, less than two weeks after the new mayoral administration was installed, David Howard was forced to resign.[1]

During a meeting with his mostly Black staff, Howard used the word *niggardly*, which is an adjective meaning "miserly, stingy, tight-fisted, or unwilling to spend money."[2] Although he used the word in reference to budgetary constraints,

African American people who heard it were outraged. The incident was reported in the news. *Niggardly*, a somewhat archaic term not in common usage, was, in their hearing, phonetically indistinguishable from *niggerly*, which is laden and rife with racial offense dating centuries back. Despite his history of harmonious engagement with the Black community, Howard's single instance of unfortunate word choice spelled his political undoing among the constituency he had so honorably served.[3]

This incident triggered anger among Black people, an outrage that was deeply felt. For many White people, however, the extent of the outrage was difficult to understand, and the consequences that Howard suffered seemed both excessive and confusing. This story is but one example of the many instances when the anger of Black people is clear, but the more deeply entrenched reasons for that anger are never exposed. Black people in Washington, D.C. were reacting to far more than Howard's use of an ill-chosen word.

In recent years, African American people have engaged in a series of widely publicized protests. Although the news reports these protests as though they are connected to single events (the Ahmaud Arbery killing, the George Floyd killing, or the Breonna Taylor killing, for example), the reasons for Black outrage are complex and go back centuries.

Think of a tree with its visible trunk, branches, and

leaves, but with extensive, invisible roots that nourish and support it. Black people have long fought for equality in America but have yet to fully achieve it. When there is an act of injustice, this reignites the frustration and outrage grounded in years and years of struggle. This outrage gets reported in the news; the roots of this outrage—invisible, underground, and extending far into the past, however—are rarely explored or acknowledged.

Unequal treatment of Black Americans based solely upon race can be traced back to the earliest colonial times. It started, very simply, with discrimination based upon skin color. This then led to slavery (1500s-1865), continued with Jim Crow segregation (1865-1960s), and was expanded through a loophole in the Thirteenth Amendment of the U.S. Constitution, leading to mass incarceration (1865-to the present day). Inequality was further enforced through *redlining*, in widespread tactics of voter suppression, and various acts of terrorism. The result of that inequality was passed from generation to generation and continues in many forms today.

I was about eight years old when I first became aware of race-based inequality. I remember well first receiving the message that there was something wrong and inferior about my brown skin. It was 1972. My family was on a much-anticipated road trip to Disney World. My parents had carefully planned and saved for this vacation, and the drive from Gary to Orlando was nearly as exciting as the destination itself. My four sisters and I passed the hours in our Station Wagon singing, playing games, arguing, and laughing as we traveled south on Interstate 65 toward the Magic Kingdom.

After several hours of driving, my father pulled into a national chain hotel somewhere in northern Georgia where we were to stay for the night. But the front desk clerk refused to serve my father. She claimed that, due to vague and inexplicable circumstances, no rooms were available. The clerk advised that he try another hotel. As she dismissed my father, he watched the same clerk welcome White customers and check them into the hotel with no questions. It was late. My father, despondent, returned to the car, where my mother had remained behind with the five of us. He explained what happened to my mother in a tone of voice that he thought was too quiet for us to hear. But we did hear. And I was just old enough to understand. That hotel would not admit us because we were Black. Feeling the weight of our dad's anger and disappointment, my sisters and I settled into silence. We merged back onto the highway and continued on to Atlanta. In the wee hours of the dark morning, we finally checked into a hotel there that welcomed us.

That early experience alerted me to the relationship between my skin color and the access to opportunities that I could expect in my life. I spent my years at Valparaiso in a state of heightened alertness, constantly swimming opposite the tide of assumptions that my brown skin triggered.

After finishing at Valparaiso University, I set out for Oklahoma to begin graduate school at the University of Tulsa. It was 1988. I'd been granted a teaching assistantship to pursue my master's degree, and having this opportunity made me feel as though I had won the lottery. Tulsa was a hybrid of small town and big city, and its main industries were oil, aerospace, and Christianity. Tulsa also had a deep and festering scar in its racial past. In 1921, it became infamous as the site of one of America's most devastating race massacres. I knew nothing about this fact when I arrived there to live.

I had been in the city a week when I stopped into one of the local grocery stores to pick up a few things on my way home from campus. Unlike cities in the north, Tulsa was a warm and friendly town, and small talk among strangers was the norm. As I stood in the checkout line, the elderly woman ahead of me turned to make conversation:

"It's busy in the store today, isn't it?" she asked, smiling at me as she spoke.

"It certainly is," I responded, noting her silver hair and powder blue ensemble. She appeared as though she had just come from church, although it was the middle of the week.

"You look nice and neat," she then said, still smiling at me.

I thought that was an odd observation. I didn't quite know

what to make of it, so I returned the smile, saying nothing.
She continued: "I need someone like you. I need help around my house with cooking, cleaning, doing my laundry, and running my errands. You look like a nice girl, and you could be a big help. Would you come and work for me?"

I can't remember how I answered her. What I remember, however, is that it was 1988. I held a bachelor's degree and had begun to pursue a master's degree. And a woman who knew only my appearance took less than five minutes to decide that I should be her maid.

African American people want to live peacefully and prosperously, just like everyone else. African American people desire a sense of purpose and they seek personal fulfillment. Driven by devotion to family and community, Black people seek out opportunities to pursue happiness and find security for themselves and those they love. When skin color presents an obstacle to doing so, there is frustration. Over time, the frustrations add up.

Black Americans want equality. While we have many successes to celebrate, the pursuit of full equality has been a long and exhausting process, expanding over many generations. Inequality has been held in place, not just by people, but by systems. While not widely known, American history includes laws and governmental practices that have inflicted harm on African American people simply because Black lives were deemed less valuable than White lives.

Some examples illustrate this point. From 1932-1972, the United States Public Health Service conducted a clinical study of the effects of untreated syphilis using as human guinea pigs 600 Black men from Macon County, Alabama. The men were led to believe that the federal government was giving them free health care. This was known as "The Tuskegee Experiment." The government had little regard for the harmful impact of this experiment on its victims or on their families or their community, an impact that extended far beyond the 600 men in question. Yet, this was made possible by the fact that Black communities, in general, were undervalued, unprotected, and at the mercy of whichever system of ethics happened to prevail at the time.[4]

From the 1920s through the 1980s, a disproportionate number of forced sterilizations, many federally financed, were performed on poor Black women in the South without their knowledge or consent. "Mississippi Appendectomy" was the nickname for this common practice in hospitals in several Southern states where medical students performed unneeded hysterectomies on Black women.[5]

The mindset at the foundation of these atrocities was forged during slavery. During the nearly 300-year antebellum period, enslaved African people were considered subhuman. They were property—living, breathing objects, each with a price tag. Their bodies were deemed valuable only to the extent that they could serve and enrich White people. When there was a need to downsize or to increase their net worth, White people routinely sold Black children away from their parents as payment for debts and routinely stripped Black husbands and wives apart from each other in pursuit of profits to bolster the bottom line. Black women were routinely raped by the White men who owned or supervised them, and these women were forced to breed with partners not of their choosing. Their bodies were subjected to multiple pregnancies from the onset of puberty until menopause, resulting in the birth of children over whom they had no say.[6]

Although modernized, the atrocities continue. The "Tuskegee Experiment" and the "Mississippi Appendectomy" are two egregious 20th-century examples of ways that Black bodies have been historically undervalued in this country. And one of many 21st-century examples was the May 25, 2020, killing of George Floyd. Minneapolis officer Derek Chauvin casually knelt on Floyd's neck for 9 minutes and 29 seconds, suffocating him to death for ultimately millions to witness.[7]

There are serious race-based inequities in the administration of American justice. Prisons are most heavily populated by people of color. This does not mean, however, that people of color are inherently more prone to crime. In *The New Jim Crow*, scholar Michelle Alexander argues persuasively that the 1980s "War on Drugs" lead to over-policing and massive arrests in Black communities.[8] A 2014 study found that Black people receive sentences that are almost ten percent longer than those of White people arrested for the same crimes.[9]

Historically, Black Americans have sought equality in employment, housing, education, in the justice system, and in the overall freedom to pursue happiness as full-fledged American citizens. Simply put, treatment that would be unthinkable for White Americans should also be unthinkable for Black Americans. If it were the case that Black Americans and all Americans enjoyed the same protections and privileges as White Americans, the anger that you see portrayed so often would disappear.

7

Why Do Black People
Seem to Want
Special Favors?

The Short Answer

If you have never gained more than a cursory knowledge of the history of Black people in America, then it may appear to you that African American people want favors or "short-cuts" simply because of their minority status. While this perception is understandable, it is inaccurate. African American people want fairness and equal opportunity to secure their lives, provide for their families, and pursue their dreams.

Imagine working for a company week after week, month after month, year after year, and never receiving a paycheck. Imagine the impact that this would have, not just on you, but on your children, and their children. Your children would miss out on decent housing, educational opportunity, and many other comforts and securities of life. Your children would inherit your poverty, and pass it on to their children, and their children, and so on. This cycle would be difficult to break because your descendants would be focused on simply trying to survive. Without an interruption to this cycle, your great, great, great grandchildren would feel the impact of the pay that you never received. In other words, the impact on your descendants could potentially last for decades, or even for centuries.

The labor of enslaved African American people was the cornerstone of the American economy for three centuries. Many people know about slavery, yet, discussions of who stood to benefit economically from slavery are largely absent from textbooks, and the subject is rarely addressed in schools. In fact, it is only recently that scholars have begun to examine the true contribution of the labor of enslaved people to America's wealth and global economic status.

If you are a White American, there is a good chance that some of the privilege that you enjoy was at least indirectly the result of the labor of enslaved people. This may be the case even if your ancestors never owned enslaved Black people themselves. For example, if you are the descendant of someone who earned a degree at an East-Coast university that was founded in the 1700s or early 1800s, it is quite likely that the labor of enslaved human beings built the buildings that housed the classrooms where your ancestor studied. If your 19th-century ancestors had warm blankets, clothing, and other household textiles, or if they profited from a business that dealt in these items, there is a very good chance that enslaved human beings picked the cotton that made these products possible.

Enslaved Black people built many government buildings, including the White House and the Capitol building. The labor of enslaved Black people built many of the structures on the campuses of prestigious colleges and universities, including Harvard University, Brown University, Emory University, University of North Carolina, and Washington & Lee University. Yale University's early major donors earned their wealth from the labor of enslaved Black people.[1] As did other institutions in antebellum America, Georgetown University sold enslaved Black people to service its debt.[2] The labor of enslaved African American people was the backbone of the cotton industry, which, simply put, made America rich. Many White Americans today are completely unaware that they are heirs to the economic benefits of slavery.

For their unpaid labor and their contribution to America's economic growth, however, African American people have neither been properly acknowledged nor properly compensated. This denial of pay has impacted many generations of Black people since slavery, through to the present day. Therefore, Black people don't want special favors; Black people simply want what's fair.

More to Consider

Slavery ended in 1865. Its impact, however, continues today. A study published by the Brookings Institute found that "At $171,000, the net worth of a typical White family" was "nearly ten times greater than that of a Black family ($17,150) in 2016. Gaps in wealth between Black and White households reveal the effects of accumulated inequality and discrimination, as well as differences in power and opportunity that can be traced back to this nation's inception."[3]

Many present-day White Americans enjoy, not just the

wealth accumulated in their own lifetimes, but the accumulated wealth of their ancestors passed to them over several generations. For roughly three centuries, slavery robbed African American people both of the time needed to accumulate wealth, and of the ability to pass wealth to multiple generations of descendants. This helps to explain the existence of the modern-day wealth gap between Black people and White people.

8

Why Can't Black People Pull Themselves Up by Their Bootstraps Like My Ancestors Did?

The Short Answer

African American people were denied many rights by both custom and law. Therefore, the metaphorical "bootstraps," in many cases, simply didn't exist. Following is one of the countless examples that illustrates how Black people have had to navigate creatively and resourcefully through life in the absence of many of the privileges that White people have always been able to take for granted.

In the early 1800s, a young Black girl was taken from her family in the Georgia Sea Islands to pick cotton on the McKee plantation in Beaufort, South Carolina. While enslaved there, she grew into womanhood, and in 1839, gave birth to a son. Enslaved women had no agency over their own bodies, so the identity of her son's father is unclear. Her son is known to history as Robert Smalls.[1]

Robert grew to be a favorite among the enslaved persons who belonged to the McKees. For this reason, when he was rented out to do various jobs in the city of Charleston, his owners allowed him to keep a small portion of his earnings. He was permitted to retain one dollar per week for himself; his owners kept the rest.

While working in Charleston Harbor, Smalls met his wife Hannah, who was also enslaved and belonged to the Kingman family. With the permission of the McKees and the Kingmans, Robert and Hannah moved into an apartment together where they had two children. They understood, however, that their marriage was tenuous, at best. At any moment, Hannah or one or both of their children could be sold to benefit the interests of their owners. They lived with the daily realization that their fate and that of their children was in the hands of others. Having saved his money over many years, Robert approached the Kingman family with an offer to buy his own wife and children. Their price, however, was far beyond what he could afford. Because he had to surrender most of his earnings to his owners, he could work the rest of his life and still not have enough money to buy his own family.

So he developed a bold and daring plan, one that, if discovered, would have cost him his life. By the time of the Civil War, Smalls had worked a number of years in Charleston Harbor. He understood all of the practices of the harbor and he was skilled in the naval operations of the Confederacy. Since he could not buy his family, he decided that he would bring them to freedom on his own. His only options were to succeed or to face certain death.

In the wee hours of the morning of May 13, 1862, Robert commandeered a Confederate ship, the *Planter*. He collected his wife and children aboard, and with his identity largely concealed by the darkness, he sailed with them past Fort Sumter toward the Union Navy fleet. He replaced the ship's Confederate flag with a white flag of surrender, and once safely beyond slave territory, the *Planter* became the property of the Union, and Robert Smalls and his family came to own themselves.

After this risky and unlikely escape, Smalls learned to read and write. Following the end of the Civil War, he returned to South Carolina, created a school for African American children, and entered politics, winning, in 1868, election to the South Carolina House of Representatives. In 1874, he was elected to the United States House of Representatives. After a colorful and productive career, he died in 1915 at age 75.

There are countless African American stories that epitomize extreme courage, ingenuity, creativity, and resourcefulness. Even during slavery and Jim-Crow segregation, there were remarkable examples of African American achievement. Many notable African American figures went from the humblest of beginnings to achieve national or international prominence. The *African American National Biography* features entries on over 4,000 African American people of note. Like Robert Smalls, many of these historical and contemporary figures elevated themselves through creative thinking and sheer grit.[2]

While Robert Smalls became legendary for his daring escape from enslavement and his illustrious political career, the questions remain: What might have Smalls become had he never been enslaved? What would have been his financial legacy to his multiple generations of descendants had he kept, saved, and invested, not just one dollar per week for the early years that he labored, but all of the money for which he worked? Furthermore, what emotional toll and psychological trauma would he and his family have been spared had he been born a White man?

More to Consider

Even generations following slavery, racial inequality persists. For this reason, it can take African American people more than twice the effort that it takes White people to self-elevate by the proverbial "bootstraps." Imagine that there are two relay teams. The race begins with the lead runner from each team at the same starting point. At the outset, it appears that they can anticipate the same challenges as well as equal opportunity to run the course and reach the finish line. The lead runner from Team #1 encounters challenges and obstacles, but he is wearing a sturdy pair of running shoes and overcomes those obstacles. For this reason, he's able to pass the baton to the next person on the relay team, who in turn, passes the baton further down the line until the finish is in sight and the race is completed.

The lead runner from Team #2, however, has his shoes forcibly removed, so he runs the same race barefoot, exposed, and vulnerable to whatever impediments to his speed are on the path before him. This fact alone makes the challenges on the course much more daunting. He runs more slowly. He cuts his feet on the rugged terrain. He has to stop and remove splinters. He has blisters. The absence of shoes makes it harder to pass the baton to the other members of the relay team even though he is running on the exact same course as the lead runner from Team #1. Because the leader of Team #2 has no shoes, and because the injuries to his feet never have time to fully heal, this impacts all of the other runners on the team who follow him, those to whom he will pass the baton.

Imagine that lead runner from Team #1 was the ancestor of a White American who migrated to America from Europe. He might have come to this country with only hope, landing perhaps at Ellis Island with little more than the clothes on his back. At first, he might have even encountered discrimination based upon his ethnicity or religion. But he had opportunity. Nothing was denied to him specifically on the basis of his skin color. Despite his humble beginnings, he was entirely free to embark on the pursuit of happiness. Perhaps he arrived at Ellis Island with a thick accent and a very ethnic surname. But he could change both his accent and his name (certainly, his children and their children would have no accent at all); and because his skin color did not distinguish him, over time, he no longer stood out as an immigrant. He could fit in.

Imagine that lead runner from Team #2 was an ancestor of a Black American who was enslaved. The enslaved ancestor and the European immigrant occupied the same country. Enslaved people, however, had far fewer rights than European immigrants. In our analogy, the denial of literacy is just one of many examples of how the "sturdy running shoes" were forcibly removed from the feet of African American people. The opportunity for literacy was stolen from enslaved people by laws that forbade them to learn to read or write. Enslaved people who learned to read (and those who taught them) were breaking the law and were dealt severe penalties, like whippings, beatings, amputations, or worst of all, being sold away from their families. The lack of literacy left many African American people vulnerable to exploitation and unequal educational opportunity that lasted for generations after slavery. Inferior education meant inferior wages, and inferior wages left little money to save or invest for building financial security for the generations that followed.[3]

While lead runner from Team #2 remained stymied by lack of literacy (not to mention many other impediments to his freedom and access to opportunity), there were no laws prohibiting his counterpart from Team #1 from learning to read. So White Americans, even those who struggled, could gain the many benefits of literacy that Black Americans— often, by law—were denied. They could also choose their own marriage partners, safeguard their families, vote in elections, have due process in court, purchase insurance, and travel to pursue opportunities, all privileges and benefits denied to African American enslaved persons and to their descendants. For European immigrants and their descendants, access to literacy (as well as access to other opportunities) paved the way for privileges, like attending colleges (many built by the labor of Black enslaved people), earning better wages, and passing some degree of financial security on to their children.

The denial of access to both literacy and the vote proved to have devastating, multigenerational impact upon African American people. During and after slavery, barriers to literacy included not only punishment for Black people who learned to read, but punishment for White people who taught them. An 1847 Virginia Criminal Code stated: "Any White person who shall assemble with slaves, [or] free negroes . . . for the purpose of instructing them to read or write, . . . shall be punished by confinement in the jail . . . and by fine . . .". Norfolk, Virginia, former slaveholder Margaret Douglass was arrested, imprisoned, and fined for teaching "free colored children" of the Christ's Church Sunday School to read and write.[4] Laws denying literacy to African American people extended well past the 19th century. In April 1916, the Florida governor ordered the arrest of three Catholic sisters, Sister Mary Thomasine Hehir, Sister Mary Scholastica Sullivan, and Sister Mary Benignus Cameron, for unlawfully educating Black children.[5]

Despite federal laws granting rights to African American people, local discriminatory practices often made those laws difficult, if not impossible to enforce. The Fifteenth

Amendment (passed by Congress in 1869 and ratified in 1870), for example, gave African American men the legal right to vote. However, in numerous states, counties, and cities, local laws were quickly enacted to make voting difficult, dangerous, or impossible for many Black people. One method of voter suppression was to charge a fee to vote which was burdensome for most African American people to pay. By the 1880s, Southern states had begun to enact the poll tax to disenfranchise Black voters. Literacy tests were also used as an intentional barrier to prevent Black people from voting. Poll taxes, literacy tests, voter intimidation, and terrorism were some of the tactics used throughout the Southern states to suppress the Black vote well into the 1960s—nearly a century after the Fifteenth Amendment was passed.[6]

Voter suppression continues. In a report by the American Civil Liberties Union posted on February 3, 2020, present-day tactics of voter suppression include strict and sometimes burdensome voter-identification laws, restricting the availability of registration, sweeping voter purges, felony disenfranchisement, and gerrymandering. These tactics have been shown to disproportionately impact Black voters. The ACLU reported, "Seventy percent of Georgia voters purged in 2018 were Black; Across the country, one in 13 Black Americans cannot vote due to disenfranchisement laws" . . . . and "counties with larger minority populations have fewer polling sites and poll workers per voter."[7] In March 2021, the state of Georgia passed a law making it illegal to give food or water to voters standing in line waiting to cast their ballots.[8]

Despite these historical and present-day barriers, African American people have shown remarkable persistence and resilience. Many African American people found safety, opportunity, self-determination, and some degree of relief from discrimination by developing and/or settling in their own all-Black or predominantly Black towns both during the antebellum period and in the late 19th and early 20th centuries. Unfortunately, racial violence inflicted by White people endangered many of these communities, sometimes leading to their demise. Following are a few of those towns (listed in no particular order) along with a brief description of each.[9]

- Fort Mose, located just north of St. Augustine, Florida, founded in 1738; abandoned in 1763;
- Rosewood, Florida, founded in 1870, population around 300. Destroyed in 1923 when a young White woman falsely accused a Black man of rape;
- Seneca Village, New York City, founded around 1825. Destroyed in 1857 with the development of Central Park;
- Greenwood, in Tulsa, Oklahoma, founded in the early 1900s, aka "Black Wall Street." Destroyed in 1921 with a White woman's accusation of assault by a Black man.

Rebuilt, thriving again by the 1940s; in decline by the late 1960s in tandem with development or "urban renewal" projects;

- Freedman's Village, Virginia, founded by the Federal Government in 1863. Located on the current site of Arlington National Cemetery, near the Pentagon. Closed by the government in 1900;
- New Philadelphia, Illinois, founded in 1836 by Kentucky former enslaved man Frank McWhorter. Declined by the 1880s;
- Blackdom, New Mexico, founded in early 1900s, peaked around 1908. Drought led to its decline in the 1920s;
- Nicodemus, Kansas, founded in 1877. Still in existence but declined to a handful of residents by 1953;
- Boley, Oklahoma, founded in 1904 on land owned by Abigail Burnett McCormick, a Black woman. Boley still exists;
- Mound Bayou, Mississippi, founded in 1887 by formerly enslaved people, under the leadership of Isaiah Montgomery, an African American man; declined, but still in existence as of 2017;
- Roberts Settlement, Hamilton County, Indiana, founded in 1835 by African American pioneers Hansel Roberts, Elijah Roberts, and Micajah Walden. In decline by the 1920s.

There are numerous examples of African American self-determination that are not widely known. Generally speaking, White people are not taught—and, therefore, have no way of knowing about—the resourcefulness, ingenuity, and persistence of Black people in the face of seemingly insurmountable circumstances.

Just a few of many examples of successful institutions, businesses, and other entities that are Black-owned and/or organized and operated include Wilberforce University, founded in 1856; North Carolina Mutual Life Insurance Company, founded in 1898 by Dr. Aaron McDuffie Moore, John Merrick, and C.C. Spaulding; Provident Hospital, founded in Chicago in 1891 by Dr. Daniel Hale Williams (currently, a public hospital; also the birthplace of former First Lady Michelle Obama); OneUnited Bank, founded in 1968 and currently headed by Kevin Cohee; *Black Enterprise Magazine*, founded in 1970 by Earl G. Graves, Jr; Black Entertainment Television (BET), founded in 1980 by Robert L. Johnson and Sheila Johnson; Brown Capital Management, founded by Eddie Brown in 1983; FUBU, an apparel manufacturer, founded in 1992 by Daymond John, Keith Perrin, J. Alexander Martin, and Carl Brown; Curls, a beauty manufacturer, founded in 2002 by Mahisha Dellinger; and McBride Sisters Collection, a winery, founded in 2005 by Robin McBride and Andrea McBride-John.[10]

9

Why Do Black Neighborhoods Often Seem Dirty, Run Down, and Dangerous?

The Short Answer

African American people live in a broad range of conditions and locations. Today, there are affluent African American communities in cities around the United States. Many Black people live in the suburbs and in well-kept middle- and upper-class neighborhoods. Still, too many African American people today reside in areas plagued by poverty, crime, and urban decay.[1] This is the case because many Black people continue to suffer from the impact of the poverty systematically imposed upon their ancestors generations ago.

I grew up in Gary, Indiana with many classmates, relatives, and family friends who lived in what some might call "dangerous" neighborhoods. These areas of the city, however, were familiar places to me and the homes of people that I knew and loved. More often than not, these homes are filled with the same love and family ties, the same dreams, and the same laughter, hope, and hard work that many value. My grandmother, for example, lived in nearby East Chicago in a neighborhood plagued by all of the ills of urban decay, and we visited her there often. I never felt the sense of danger that the media often associates with people who have few resources. There is a tendency to over-police and over-report when tragic incidents occur in these communities. By comparison, there is little to no coverage of the successes and celebrations that these communities enjoy.

Poor neighborhoods do not suffer because they are

populated by Black people and other people of color. Instead, these communities suffer because of long-standing, federally supported practices that now trap their citizens in economic stagnation. And it started nearly a century ago.

In the 1930s, the Federal Housing Authority implemented a segregated housing practice called *redlining*. Color-coded maps in almost every major metropolitan area showed White areas where the FHA would insure mortgages, and Black areas where it would not. This practice created a barrier to homeownership based entirely upon skin color. At the same time that the FHA subsidized large numbers of suburban mortgages for middle-class White families, it subsidized no mortgages in Black communities, citing—with no evidence aside from racial stereotypes—risk of loss in property value. This practice—which was legal, commonplace, and a federally-supported custom—restricted Black people to inner-cities where they became rent-paying tenants rather than homeowners.[2]

As perpetual tenants, many African American people were trapped. They were at the mercy of landlords who were free to manipulate the price of rents. Landlords also have had varying degrees of interest in maintaining their property. Even after the practice of redlining was no longer commonplace, its effects remained for generations. By excluding many African American people from the opportunity to make the fundamental investment in home ownership, they were kept out of the middle class, and prevented from owning property that could be passed to their children. A population thus trapped, with little to no disposable income, must overcome unbelievable odds to envision a life beyond survival.[3]

More to Consider

The phrase "Black-on-Black Crime" has been used to underscore inner-city violence where both the perpetrators and their victims are African American people. This use of language is problematic, however, because there are no corresponding descriptions of violent crime associated with other races. The Oklahoma City bombing of 1995, the Columbine High School massacre of 1999, the Sandy Hook School shooting of 2012, and the Aurora, Colorado, theatre shooting, also of 2012, were carried out by White Americans, and their victims were overwhelmingly White. Yet, references to "White-on-White Crime" were not used. In fact, the coverage of these stories in the news rarely invoked race at all in characterizing those tragedies. Instead, these incidents are often treated as isolated, unlikely, and the result of someone who was mentally or emotionally disturbed. Using race at all to label violent crime distracts from the sad fact that all are vulnerable. Furthermore, racialized descriptions of crime distract from an understanding of the conditions that can place anyone, regardless of race, on the path leading to criminal behavior.

Neighborhood crime has never been a product of race. Instead, neighborhood crime is more prevalent where economic opportunities are rare, where resources are limited, and where, because of these circumstances, the primary focus must be on survival. Patterns of over-policing and police brutality in some disadvantaged neighborhoods have created a sense of distrust in law enforcement. In some cases, this further complicates strategies to deal with crime when it occurs.

The media commonly associates inner-city crime with Black gang violence. Before the spotlight turned to African Americans, however, White inner-city gangs were quite common (the 1961 musical, *West Side Story*, although fictional, dramatizes this fact).[4] Early scholarship on street gangs found that socio-economic status, not race, was the primary determinant of the number and nature of crimes committed. For example, a 1966 study of inner-city crime and violence examined behaviors of both White and African American gangs. That particular study found that in similar-status Black and White street gangs, "racial differences were relatively unimportant," and that White people rather than Black people were more likely both to engage in and to be arrested for violent crimes. White gang members engaged in field-recorded acts of illegal violence "twice as often" as Black gang members.[5] A 1969 study found that gangs were a phenomenon in both small towns and big cities, and small-town gangs included both groups that were White and groups that were Black.[6] American history therefore proves that, regardless of race, gangs attract groups with the least economic opportunity and the greatest need for connections that will afford them a sense of status and belonging.

White Americans, many of them immigrants from Europe, were the original occupants of many of the areas that today are commonly described as the "inner city." But as White people were able to get long-term, low-interest, little-money-down mortgages for the first time in U.S. history, they were no longer confined to these areas. They were able to venture out into locations that were safer, more comfortable, and with more family-friendly green space and options for recreation and education. Too many African American people and their descendants, however, remained indefinitely confined to rental situations, thanks, in large part, to the legacy of discriminatory mortgage lending practices.

10

Am I a Racist if I Prefer to Be With My Own Kind?

The Short Answer

You are not racist if you prefer to be with your own kind. It is human nature for us to feel at ease with those who are most like us. Most of us enjoy spending time with those whose experiences and perspectives we share.

Studies have shown that there is a natural, human tendency for people to privilege their own. Even in the absence of conscious racial hostility, we all tend to privilege both what we know and who we know. Said another way, we pick for our team those who seem most like us. This fact is supported by the results of an experiment conducted around 2007 by Rebecca Bigler in Austin, Texas with young children. In their *Newsweek* article "Even Babies Discriminate," Po Bronson and Ashley Merryman show how easily even very young children develop "in-group preferences." They describe an experiment involving three preschool classrooms, in which 4- and 5-year-olds were lined up and given T-shirts. They write:

> Half the kids were randomly given blue T-shirts, half red. The children wore the shirts for three weeks. During that time, the teachers never mentioned their colors and never grouped the kids by shirt color. . . . The kids didn't segregate in their behavior. They played with each other freely at recess. But when asked which color

team was better to belong to, or which team might win a race, they chose their own color. They believed they were smarter than the other color. "The Reds never showed hatred for Blues," Bigler observed. "It was more like, 'Blues are fine, but not as good as us.'" When Reds were asked how many Reds were nice, they'd answer, "All of us." Asked how many Blues were nice, they'd answer, "Some." Some of the Blues were mean, and some were dumb—but not the Reds.[1]

We all tend to pick those most like us to be on our team. And like the children in the experiment, we all have a natural tendency to think most highly of those with whom we most strongly identify. You might consider, however, whether skin color alone (as opposed to character, common interests, common values, etc.) is the primary factor determining your social circle.

More to Consider
If your entire social circle consists solely of members of your own race, you may be somewhat detached from reality and behind the times. According to William H. Frey, author of *Diversity Explosion: How New Racial Demographics are Remaking America* (2018), White Americans will become the minority by 2045.[2] Census trends project that White people

will comprise 49.7% of the American population by that year and will be outnumbered by people of color, including Hispanic people, Black people, Asian people, and people who identify as multiracial. In June 2019, the Brookings Institute reported that, "For the first time, non-Hispanic White residents now make up less than half (49.9%) of the nation's under age 15 population. . . .".[3]

There are many White people who have friendships with people of color, but they are intentionally discreet about these relationships. Perhaps they fear the reactions of their White peers; or maybe they struggle internally with the mismatch between the authenticity of these friendships and their own inherited, deeply ingrained notions about race. Because of the racist norms of this country, many White Americans have lived double lives. They have appeared to navigate freely among White family and peers in public but have kept the secret truths of their relationships with African American people quite private. A striking example of this is the paradoxical life of long-time Senator Strom Thurmond of South Carolina. In public, Thurmond was an ardent segregationist and voted against both the Civil Rights Act of 1964 and the Voting Rights Act of 1965. He was known for his embrace of White supremacy and his opposition to equality for African American people, and he argued vehemently during the years of the Civil Rights Movement that the races should remain separate. Yet, his private life was misaligned with his public persona. He fathered a daughter with his family's then 16-year-old Black maid, Carrie Butler. Thurmond had a lifelong connection with his daughter, Essie Mae Washington-Williams. She revealed her father's identity after his death at age 100 in 2003. Thurmond harbored this secret for the 48 years that he served in Congress.[4]

Today, interracial relationships and families are becoming increasingly normalized. According to the Pew Research Center, interracial marriages and families have steadily increased since 1967, with 17% of those married in 2015 wedding someone of a different race or ethnicity. Survey results from Pew also indicate that attitudes about interracial marriage have evolved in tandem with this increase, with opposition most heavily concentrated among older adults, and acceptance of interracial marriage most heavily concentrated among younger adults.[5]

Therefore, while maintaining an exclusively White social circle is not intrinsically racist, it does almost guarantee that you will remain out of touch with an increasingly diverse and globalized society.

11

Am I a Racist for Wanting
to Keep Crime Out of
My Safe and Peaceful
Community?

The Short Answer

No one wants to live in a crime-ridden neighborhood. We all want to be safe. The belief that the presence of Black people = the presence of crime, however, is an inaccurate and racist assumption. Black people are accused of more crimes than White people, but Black people don't necessarily commit more crimes. The narrative about the criminal nature of Black people was created over 150 years ago. And it had everything to do with money. As early as 1865, criminalizing Black people became a way to ensure that White people had access to free Black labor even after slavery was abolished.

The end of slavery dealt a devastating blow to the economy, and to the Southern economy, in particular, because it meant that the free labor available for more than the prior two centuries abruptly disappeared. How would the South have any hope of economic survival when millions of formerly enslaved persons suddenly had to be paid for their work?

In 1865, the Thirteenth Amendment abolished slavery. The drafters of the amendment, however, added a very significant loophole. It reads as follows (emphasis added):

> *Neither slavery nor involuntary servitude, **<u>except</u>
> <u>as a punishment for crime whereof the party</u>
> <u>shall have been duly convicted</u>, shall exist
> within the United States, or any place subject to*

their jurisdiction.

The portion underlined and in boldface proved devastating for African American people and is still felt today. With the abrupt loss of the entire free labor force, this loophole in the Thirteenth Amendment created a legal way to recover some of the free labor that the abolition of slavery had taken away. Said another way, it literally incentivized White people to think of Black people as criminals—potential convicts who could then be legally forced to work for free.

Laws were created around the South that made it easy to convict Black people for frivolous "crimes," regardless of whether or not there was actual evidence of criminal activity. As early as 1866, shortly after the passage of the Thirteenth Amendment, many Southern states began to enact vagrancy laws. These laws made it a crime to be homeless and unemployed. Untold numbers of Black people were arrested, convicted of violating vagrancy laws, and forced into unpaid labor as punishment for this "crime," thus returning to Southern White people some of the free labor lost with the abolition of slavery.

The loophole in the Thirteenth Amendment made it profitable for many to assume that Black people were criminals. The assumption that Black people are guilty until proven innocent was then passed from generation to generation and persists today.[1] Ample evidence indicates that this assumption broadly impacts the American criminal justice system. In her 2018 study of racial bias in criminal court decisions, Lydette Assefa found that " the use of pretrial detention disproportionately affects black defendants who are more likely to receive higher bond amounts and more restrictive conditions than white defendants facing similar charges." She found further that "Bond decisions are particularly susceptible to implicit bias because they often require judges to make quick, on-the-spot, complex, and predictive decisions about a defendant's threat to the community and likelihood to reappear in court. These decisions occur when judges have very limited information about the individual defendant, leading to a misguided reliance on racial stereotypes." She cites the following statistics that are especially telling:

> Black defendants are detained pretrial at higher rates, yet research has found that white defendants are more likely to be rearrested for new crimes committed during the pretrial period, providing convincing evidence of racial bias against black defendants in bond decisions. Marginally released white defendants are 22.2 percentage points more likely to be rearrested prior to case disposition than marginally released black defendants. . . . The higher arrest

rates for white defendants transcend all crime types. . . . Marginally released white defendants are 8 percentage points more likely to be rearrested for a violent crime, 4.7 percentage points more likely to be rearrested for a drug crime, and 16.3 percentage points more likely to be rearrested for a property crime prior to case disposition than marginally released black defendants. . . . The significant incongruity between release rates and rearrest rates for black and white defendants suggests that judges are likely racially biased against black defendants and highlights the inaccuracies in the current risk-assessment system at the expense of black defendants.[2]

More to Consider

In 1989, five Black teenagers (Korey Wise, Kevin Richardson, Raymond Santana, Antron McCray, and Yusef Salaam, a.k.a. the "Central Park Five") were arrested for the rape and assault of a White female jogger in Central Park. The youngsters were convicted based partly on police-coerced confessions, and collectively, spent between six and 13-plus years in prison for the crimes. Before the trial, Donald Trump spent $85,000 on full-page ads in New York newspapers calling for the death penalty. After years in prison, the five youngsters were proven innocent of the crimes to which convicted murderer and serial rapist Matias Reyes later confessed. (See dramatization in the Netflix Film, *When They See Us*.) As of this writing, Donald Trump has never apologized for the false accusation against these five innocent young men.[3]

In 1995, South Carolina mother Susan Smith reported her two children missing. She fanned the racial tensions of her community and attracted international attention when she told police that a Black man had carjacked her and kidnapped her young sons. Her tearful, televised plea for their return triggered outrage against the unidentified Black man and garnered the sympathy she appeared to deserve. Within two weeks, however, Susan Smith admitted that her story was fabricated. Smith herself had murdered her three-year-old and her toddler by strapping them into their car seats inside of the Mazda that she then allowed to roll into the lake.[4]

In 2018, two African American men were arrested and removed in handcuffs from a Philadelphia-area Starbucks. The two men were there waiting on a friend to join them. An employee, assuming the Black men to be suspicious, called the police, shortly after which six Philadelphia police officers arrived and asked them to leave. Although they had done nothing wrong, the men were arrested, taken into custody, and detained for several hours. It turns out that the three friends had planned to meet at Starbucks to discuss a real estate deal.[5]

Also in 2018, Jermaine Massey was on the phone in the lobby of a Doubletree Hotel in Portland, Oregon. A guard approached him, interrupted his call, and demanded to know whether he was a guest in the hotel. Massey confirmed that he was a guest. The guard further demanded his room number and that he produce a room key. The guard then accused him of loitering and endangering the security of the guests, and he summoned the manager. Police came and escorted Massey from the hotel. Humiliated in front of the other guests who witnessed his arrest, Massey later filed suit for $10 million. Massey, an African American man, was on the phone with his mother.[6]

On May 25, 2020, Christian Cooper, a Black man who was birdwatching in Central Park, became distracted by a dog that was nearby running loose. The dog belonged to Amy Cooper (no relation), a White woman. When Cooper asked Ms. Cooper to restrain her dog, she became irate, pulled out her cell phone, and threatened him. Mr. Cooper then began to record her: "I'm taking a picture and calling the cops," she said . . . . "I'm going to tell them there's an African American man threatening my life." She then called the police and reported that Cooper was threatening her and her dog. His recording of the incident became a national headline and Amy Cooper was charged with filing a false police report.[7]

On September 25, 2020, the *Washington Post* reported that 9-year-old Ka Mauri Harrison, an African American boy attending school online, faced expulsion when his fourth-grade teacher spotted a toy BB gun in his bedroom. The punishment was reduced from expulsion to suspension, but the incident alters his record. The same article reports that in August 2020, a Colorado school called police on an African American seventh grader for handling a toy gun during an online class.[8]

The false accusations of Trump, Smith, the Starbucks employee, the Doubletree security guard, Amy Cooper, and the frivolous reports of the online teachers are representative of the countless cases where the public has proven its inclination to assume the guilt of African American people. Black males of all ages are especially vulnerable to false accusations. The stigma remains even after they are later proven to have done no wrong.

Ample research shows the impact of race and racism upon the way teachers perceive students, even as early as preschool. A 2003 study showed that White teachers perceived Black male students who exhibited "Black" movements and used "Black" slang to be aggressive, academically low-achieving, and more in need of special education.[9]

In 2016, Dr. Walter S. Gilliam of the Yale University Child Study Center found that preschool teachers had a higher expectation of problem behavior from Black boys than from other children and were more likely to recommend Black students for disciplinary action, including expulsion. From the abstract:

Participants . . . completed two tasks. In Task 1, participants were primed to expect challenging behaviors (although none were present) while watching a video of preschoolers . . . as the participants' eye gazes were tracked. In Task 2, participants read a standardized vignette of a preschooler with challenging behavior and were randomized to receive the vignette with the child's name implying either a Black boy, Black girl, White boy, or White girl . . . . Findings revealed that when expecting challenging behaviors teachers gazed longer at Black children, especially Black boys.[10]

Harvard Sociology Professor Ellis Monk collected data between 2001 and 2003 which showed a direct correlation between skin color and the likelihood of being arrested. These findings were included in a 2019 article published by Yahoo News titled "The Darker Your Skin, the More Likely You'll End up in an American Jail," by Annalisa Merelli.[11]

Given the assumption that Black people are, by nature, more prone than others to criminal behavior, it is no surprise that, on average, a Black man will receive a sentence that is almost 10% longer than a White man convicted of the same crime.[12]

While Black men seem most often to be the subjects of unwarranted suspicion, Black women are also often treated as guilty before proven innocent. I recall a particular instance of being treated with suspicion in my search for housing as a college student. In the summer of 1989 prior to my second year of grad school, I went looking for an apartment in Tulsa, hoping to get settled in for the start of the fall semester. I found an attractive complex that was a short drive to campus and conveniently situated near an array of interesting shops and restaurants. Best yet, it was in my price range.

I went to the rental office to inquire about availability, with excellent credit, gainful employment, money in the bank, and a down payment in hand. Although the property manager said that there were vacancies, she was less than welcoming: "You don't want to live here," were her exact words to me. She encouraged me to look elsewhere, explaining to me, without any evidence, that she didn't believe I could afford it and that she was sure I'd be happier elsewhere. Needless to say, I got her message and left to pursue other options.

Like many African American people, I have been treated with suspicion while shopping. My most awkward experiences have been at clothing stores. When browsing, I have been followed at uncomfortably close range by salesclerks offering repeatedly to help me, although nothing in my behavior or expression indicates a need for help. At times, salesclerks have asked, "Are you going to buy that?" even before I've had the chance to go to a fitting room and try on the article.

If you live in a safe, peaceful, all-White neighborhood, there is no evidence that your surroundings will become less safe if your neighbors are people of color. I grew up in a loving home on a beautiful street in all-Black Gary, Indiana. I felt completely safe there the entire time and don't recall any cases of theft, vandalism, or violent crime in my neighborhood. I have been a homeowner in racially integrated neighborhoods now for nearly thirty years where all indications have been that everyone shares the same interest in the wellbeing of the community.

12

Why Do Black People Get Away With Saying The "N" Word When White People Cannot?

The Short Answer

It is a fact that some African American entertainers use the "N" word freely, while White people who use it are often dealt severe penalties for doing so. It is understandable that this would be confusing.

In August 2010, celebrity talk radio host Dr. Laura Schlessinger (popularly known as "Dr. Laura") took a call from the Black wife in an interracial marriage who was distressed at her husband's dismissal of his friends' racist remarks. Dr. Laura derided the caller for being hypersensitive, pointing out that Black comics on HBO, and famous Black rappers and other entertainers, use the "N" word all the time. To make her point, and to ask what the big deal was, Dr. Laura repeated the "N" word several times in rapid succession for her national radio audience to hear. She asserted that if Black people could use the "N" word, then she should be able to use it as well, and why should anyone find this offensive(?). It was 2010, and Dr. Laura further lamented that even with a Black president, there was "more complaining than ever" from Black people. That broadcast went viral, sparking quite the firestorm. Dr. Laura lost sponsorship, and within days, resigned from her radio show.[1]

Buried within her offensive remarks, and hidden within its painful impact, was a very legitimate question: *"If the 'N' word is so offensive, why do Black people themselves use it?"*
I suspect that somewhere in her heart, Dr. Laura really wanted to know the answer.

Here's an analogy that may help to explain why this term is so problematic for White people to use: Imagine that your two legs are exactly the same, except that one is encumbered and the other is not. One leg is free and flexible with the ability to bend and move and dance however it wills. The other leg, however, is bound by a 400-lb ball and chain that is excruciatingly painful to drag along. Every effort to move that leg is a reminder of all that burdens, oppresses, and constricts it.

The "N" word is linguistically unique in this country in that it derives its meaning most powerfully, not from inflection or context, but from the person who says it. When African American people use the "N" word, it is completely deracialized. The sting and the poison are absent. When spoken by Black people, the "N" word can have a range of meanings and can even be a light-hearted term of endearment. It is a norm of African American culture to redefine and repurpose, and this is evident in our cuisine, in the way we do religion, certainly in our music, and in our use of language—whatever is at hand to serve creative or expressive function. In the same way that we have transformed pig intestines into a coveted delicacy (called "chitterlings" and typically pronounced "chitlins"), language has also been at our disposal to flip on its head, turn inside out, and make it mean what we want. That freedom and versatility in African American expression is like the flexibility and fluidity of the unencumbered leg in our two-leg analogy.

When someone White utters the "N" word, by contrast, its meaning instantly transforms. When spoken by a White voice, the "N" word automatically triggers the 400-year history of oppression at the hands of White hegemony and the resulting inequality that persists through to the present day. Upon White utterance, the "N" word connects to the brutality of bondage and the heartbreak of families splintered and spouses and children bought and sold as chattel during slavery. White usage of the "N" word is associated with Jim Crow segregation that persisted through the 1960s, with the discriminatory practice of redlining in real estate, with lynching, and with mass incarceration. White people who use that word instantly remind us of police brutality, voter suppression, and other painful realities of the past four centuries, the impacts of which are felt today. That's the other leg in our two-leg analogy, the one bound by the heavy ball and chain. This is why use of the "N" word by White people is so problematic and hurtful.

As I performed with the marching band on Valparaiso's main street, I flinched internally upon hearing the spectator call out, "Hey, look at the nigger!" His intent was to identify, isolate, humiliate, and heckle me by drawing public attention to the color of my skin. His use of the "N" word was his way of putting me on notice, reminding me that I was unwelcome in that city despite the fact that I was a part of the band and a student in good standing at the University. And he succeeded. After that day, I never ventured into downtown Valparaiso again.

More to Consider

The etymology of the word *nigger* goes back to the late 16th century and descends from *niger*, the Latin word for the color black. Cognates include the Spanish *negro*, the French *nègre*, and the early English *neger*, all of which refer to the color black.

Negative characteristics associated with dark or Black skin date back several centuries, and these were reinforced by the Catholic Church. In June 1452, Pope Nicholas V issued a papal bull known as *Dum Diversas*, which authorized Spain and Portugal to enslave Africans:

> We grant you [Kings of Spain and Portugal] by these present documents, with our Apostolic Authority, full and free permission to invade, search out, capture, and subjugate the Saracens and pagans and any other unbelievers and enemies of Christ wherever they may be, as well as their kingdoms, duchies, counties, principalities, and other property [...] and to reduce their persons into perpetual servitude.[2]

The word *Saracen* meant Muslim, and the Muslims referred to in this context were mostly Africans. The primary justification cited for enslaving these people was religious, not racial. The motivation for enslaving these "unbelievers and enemies of Christ," of course, was gold.

Several of Pope Nicholas V's successors issued their own reinforcements of *Dum Diversas*, providing an authoritative, religious basis for the argument that the pagans should be captured and subdued for the purpose of Christianizing them, the "necessary" remedy for their "innate, barbaric" nature.

Before the mid-1600s, our modern-day notion of *race* as defined by skin color and other physical characteristics did not exist. The term *race* simply referred to categories of people based upon any number of possible characteristics— social, political, professional, or otherwise. David Roediger writes:

> European colonists' use of the word "white" to refer to people who looked like themselves, grew to become entangled with the word "race" and "slave" in the American colonies in the mid-1660s. These elites created "races" of "savage" Indians, "subhuman" Africans, and "white" men. The social inventions succeeded in uniting the white colonists, dispossessing and

marginalizing native people, and permanently enslaving most African-descended people for generations.[3]

The European colonists, therefore, purposefully started the practice of categorizing people according to physical appearance, conflating the notion of race with skin color and infusing their own ideas of superiority and inferiority into this new type of classification. This enabled them to both identify and justify the use of people for much-needed labor based upon the color of their skin.

Until the end of the 17th century, Europeans considered African people to be inferior and prime for capture and enslavement primarily on the basis of religion; they were pagans who needed the "correction" of Christianity. By the early 18th century, however, Colonial America was embracing the newly invented idea that Black people were also inferior because of their darker skin. Printed in Boston in 1706, the pamphlet "The Negro Christianized," for example, describes the ghastly and repulsive nature of Black people in their natural state and proposes Christianity to correct this. The following quote makes particular reference, however, to the "Blackened" skin of the unconverted African people:

Let not this opportunity be lost . . . but make a trial, whether by your means, the most Brutish

> creatures upon Earth...may not come to be
> disposed . . . like the Angels of Heaven. . . . Let
> us make a trial, whether they that have been
> scorched and Blacken'd by the Sun of Africa,
> may not come to have their Minds Healed by . . .
> the Sun of Righteousness.[4]

As the African population in America increased, so did the need for narratives and justifications for the particularly brutal brand of slavery practiced in the New World. Skin color made it easy to identify and subjugate this specific group of people, these savages, called *negars*, *negroes*, and ultimately *niggers.*

In America, enslaved Africans were property in the truest sense, objects at the complete mercy and disposal of their masters. Enslaved men and women had no rights to their own bodies. Enslaved women were routinely raped or forced to "breed" with their owners and/or with other enslaved persons for the purpose of producing children to increase the net worth of the landowner. Enslaved Black people often selected spouses, but these partnerships were tenuous at best. Pairings required the approval of the master, and forbidden liaisons could be met with severe punishment. They could not legally marry, and romantic commitments between enslaved persons did nothing to prevent enslaved spouses from being sexually available to their White masters at all times. Enslaved families were routinely fragmented, as husbands, wives, or children could be sold at will, often to settle the debts of their owners. Typically, enslaved Black people were forbidden to learn to read, were forbidden to gather without White supervision (although they did), and were forbidden to own property. Enslaved Black people were often rented out to perform labor for which their masters were paid. In some cases, enslaved persons were allowed to keep their earnings and eventually buy their own freedom. Legally, however, both the enslaved and everything in their possession—from their bodies, to their children, to their names, to any wages of their own earning—were the property of the White landowner.

By the early 1800s, the term *nigger* had evolved in its connotation to become decidedly pejorative, meaning not only Black (in reference to skin color), but also Black persons who, by virtue of their Blackness, were deemed intrinsically inferior, barbaric, despicable, crude, dirty, and primitive. Randall Kennedy writes:

> In *A Treatise on the Intellectual Character and Civil and Political Condition of the Colored People of the United States: and the Prejudice Exercised Towards Them* (1837), Hosea Easton wrote that *nigger* 'is an opprobrious term, employed to impose contempt upon [Black people] as an

inferior race. . . . The term in itself would be perfectly harmless were it used only to distinguish one class of society from another; but it is not used with that intent. . . . [I]t flows from the fountain of purpose to injure.' Easton averred that often the earliest instruction White adults gave to White children prominently featured the word *nigger*. Adults reprimanded them for being 'worse than niggers,' for being '*ignorant as niggers*,' for having '*no more credit than niggers*;' they disciplined them by telling them that unless they behaved they would be carried off by '*the old nigger*' or made to sit with '*niggers*' or consigned to the '*nigger seat*,' which was, of course, a place of shame.[5]

This history helps to explain why White usage of the term *nigger* is inextricably linked to a centuries-old history of systematic oppression. Therefore, when used by White people, the term is highly offensive.

Today, use of the "N" word is further complicated by its prevalence in the language of popular culture. Many youngsters—both Black youngsters and White youngsters—are detached from the problematic history of this word. They casually use the "N" word as a nickname for their friends, or they sing it as it occurs in the lyrics of popular tunes. For many of them, the term is a deracialized component of the slang they use every day, and offense is neither intended nor perceived. When this occurs in my hearing, however, I find open doors to inform and educate.

Here's an example. When a relative of mine was in high school, he dated a White girl who joined our family for dinner one evening. She was a lovely young woman—bubbly, outgoing, attractive, and articulate. In what was clearly intended in a lighthearted way, she referred to him as her "nigger." Instantly, the atmosphere became awkward and uncomfortable. And she was clearly confused as to the sudden change in the room.

I motioned for her to join me outside, away from the family, and I asked if she and I could have a chat. I explained to her the history of the term, the pain it triggered for many adults my age and older, and why her use of the word was especially off-putting. She was shocked, but gracious and receptive, and she understood that my intent was not to penalize her, but to inform her. She was embarrassed and remorseful, but I forgave her, embraced her, and we returned to resume our dinner.

Language matters. While teaching moments like this won't always be possible, it is important to inform and enlighten whenever there are opportunities to do so.

13

Why Do Black People Continue to Complain Even After the Election of Barack Obama?

The Short Answer

Many consider the election of Barack Obama in 2008 (and his reelection in 2012) to be an important milestone of racial progress in America. President Obama's election, however, did not solve systemic racism. In fact, it exposed existing, latent racial tensions leading to an escalation of hateful and discriminatory acts. Reuters reported that the election of Obama provoked a rise in hate crimes.[1] Similarly, on November 25, 2008, National Public Radio reported, "In the few weeks since Election Day, cross burnings, racist graffiti, and other alleged hate crimes have been reported."[2]

Barack Obama was distinguished as both the first African American president and the only president whose American citizenship was challenged in a series of ongoing, highly publicized legal and political gestures that predated his presidency and continued for nearly his entire time in the White House. In 2004, Illinois politician Andy Martin became the first to suggest that Obama was not an American citizen. In 2008, Clinton supporters circulated emails questioning Obama's citizenship, which ultimately forced Obama to publicly release (for the first of at least two times) his birth certificate. That same year, a series of lawsuits were filed challenging Obama's eligibility for the presidency, based upon doubtful citizenship. In 2009, a highly publicized Kenyan birth certificate, purported to be Obama's, appeared in the media and on eBay. In April 2011, Obama released his long-form birth certificate. Despite this, from 2011 to 2016, Donald Trump led the "Birtherism" charge, questioning Obama's citizenship repeatedly during televised interviews, and encouraging his base to do the same. Finally, in September 2016, Trump sheepishly conceded that Obama was born in the United States of America.[3]

Obama's presidency, therefore, was both an important first and a painful reminder that if you are a brown person in this country, you can ascend even to the presidency and still be viewed by many as unworthy, inadequate, and an imposter.

More to Consider

On October 7, 2020, Karen Tumulty, Kate Woodsome, and Sergio Pecanha published an op-ed in the *Washington Post* titled, "How Sexist, Racist Attacks on Kamala Harris Have Spread Online—A Case Study." Like Obama, Kamala Harris became an African American first, making history in November 2020 when she was confirmed Vice President-elect, slated to serve alongside then President-elect Joe Biden.[4]

In the United States, it has often been the case that when African American people ascend to levels of prominence or national leadership, they face attacks that ignore fact-based critiques of their qualifications or credentials. Instead, these attacks are often based upon negative stereotypes related to race.

A familiar weapon wielded against female leaders, and particularly against female leaders of color, is the accusation that they somehow slept their way to the top. Kamala Harris holds degrees in political science, economics, and law. She served as deputy district attorney, then as district attorney, and was elected as attorney general for the state of California before becoming a U.S. senator. Despite her experience and credentials, however, she faces accusations, as did Obama, of failing to meet the requirement of U.S. citizenship. Furthermore, she has also been accused of trading sexual favors in exchange for her rise in the political arena.[5]

Labeling Black people as incompetent and oversexualized is a common tactic of oppression. One need not be on the national stage to experience this most unsavory of race- and gender-based character attacks. In my junior year at Valpo, I took a course in communications, and as was usually the case, I was the lone African American student in the class. The course was designed to generate group and class discussions on a series of heated and controversial topics as a way to develop skills in effective speech. Today, academic institutions take much greater care in monitoring topics that may trigger trauma for students. Back in the mid-1980s, however, no one cared about triggers. Any topic was fair game.

On this particular day, the topic was date rape. The

instructor sectioned the class of about 40 students off into groups. After initial discussion within the smaller groups, she then reconvened the class for reporting out. It was during this portion of the hour that one of the White male students who had been in my smaller group directed a question to me for the entire class to hear:

"Teresa, would you rather be raped by a Black man or by a White man?" he asked, looking me directly in the face, waiting for me to answer this most ludicrous and humiliating of questions, a question clearly reserved for me and for no one else.

Everyone in the class—including the professor—fell silent and awaited my response. They were curious to see how I would answer a question which was itself embedded with the assumption that rape was something that someone who looked like me would welcome. The question itself made me feel violated, exposed, and thoroughly disrespected. And the only authority figure in the room, the professor, was ill-equipped to point out the inappropriateness of the question and come to my defense.

My answer was simple, direct, and emphatic: "I would prefer not to be raped at all."

My classmate knew exactly what he was doing. By asking me a question that framed me as inherently oversexualized, he shifted the focus from my academic worthiness (I was known to be one of the top students in the class) to the race-

and gender-based stereotypes that best aligned with his own values and perspective. He was more comfortable seeing me as a stereotype than as his peer, so the question he posed was his rhetorical weapon of choice.

The experiences of President Obama and now Vice President Harris underscore the fact that successful people of color are often "taxed" for their success. They must use their time, mental resources, and emotional energy to endure, address, and deflect various race- and/or gender-based challenges to their competence and legitimacy.

The success "tax" is layered on top of all of the other requirements that successful Black people must fulfill in order to remain effective in their roles. President Obama still had to run the country while answering Birtherism charges; he could not take time off from his work to process those baseless and hurtful accusations. Vice President Harris can't take a "time out" to heal from the attacks on her character. And I had to continue showing up for class every Monday, Wednesday, and Friday for the remainder of the semester. Even though my classmate attached an undesirable stigma to me, my responsibility for meeting the requirements of the course remained unchanged.

Because of his brown skin, Barack Obama experienced the presidency very differently than all of his predecessors. As the United States transforms to become populated primarily by people of color, diversity in every stratum of leadership hopefully will become the norm.

14

Why Do I Feel Threatened by Successful Black People?

The Short Answer

Perhaps you have an unconscious assumption that Black people should be unsuccessful. Therefore, when you encounter someone who challenges that assumption, it feels confusing and uncomfortable to you.

We are all the products of what we are taught. If you have received negative messages about African American people your entire life, then you are likely to assume that these negative stereotypes are factual. If you grew up in a family that viewed African American people in a negative way, it would stand to reason that you would share those views. If the books you read and the lessons you were taught in school failed to present African American successes and achievements, then you might have no awareness that these successes and achievements exist. If the authority figures in your life were uncomfortable around Black people, they likely passed that discomfort on to you in some way.

More to Consider

More than a century ago, colleges and universities began to teach that Black people were inherently inferior. A new field of scholarship gained popularity in the early 1900s that purported to explain racial inferiority in terms of legitimate science. The then emerging field of *eugenics* used Darwinian notions of "survival of the fittest" to support and justify assessments of human value based entirely upon race. From this perspective, Black people were illiterate, poor, and disproportionately given to crime because they were inherently inferior; they were inferior because they were illiterate, poor, and disproportionately given to crime. This flawed, circular logic ignored the fact that the majority of African American people were mismatched to this model. Furthermore, it completely failed to acknowledge the impact of oppressive systems or institutionalized barriers to upward mobility for people of color.[1]

In 1914, Charles H. McCord published what was then considered to be a scholarly textbook titled *The American Negro as a Dependent, Defective, and Delinquent*. Following are quotes from that text. In an "analysis" of African people based entirely upon ill-founded assumption and biased observation, the writer made these seemingly authoritative claims:

"The West African is intensely religious, but his religion is non-moral and more dreadful than comforting . . . . Out of his religion grow many absurd practices . . . . "

"The West African is improvident and wasteful. He never looks out for the future...."

"He is shiftless and lazy and lacks ambition. . . ."

"He is impulsive and lacking in inhibitive power. He cannot restrain his lips from laughter nor his hands from bloodshed."

"He is volatile, excitable, and demonstrative, but is incapable of sustained effort, either mental or physical."[2]

The academic tone of writings like this gave legitimacy to their assertions, even when faulty premises were the basis of their claims. A powerful shaping force in the early 20th-century American mindset, *eugenics* gave academic legitimacy to the practice of broadly categorizing entire populations in terms of imagined standards of quality and purity. By today's norms, the "science" used to claim that Black people were inherently inferior would never pass muster. Yet, in the early 1900s, many took the assertions of writers like Charles H. McCord seriously, and they took eugenics as truth. Elements of these devastating and inaccurate messages about race have persisted through to the present day, shaping expectations and assumptions about people of color.

The media is a powerful teacher and can often send messages that create broadly held assumptions. Historically, the portrayal of African American people in the media has emphasized negative traits more often than positive ones. In a recent study, researchers reviewed more than 800 local and national news stories published or aired between January 2015 and December 2016, randomly sampling features on ABC, CBS, NBC, CNN, Fox News and MSNBC, as well as in *The Washington Post, Wall Street Journal, The New York Times, USA Today, Los Angeles Times,* and *Chicago Tribune.* They also reviewed regional newspapers, conservative websites such as Breitbart, and Christian news sources like the *Christian Post.* The study concluded that, overall, news sources furthered false narratives about Black families. Black families represented 59% of the poor portrayed in the media, according to the analysis, but accounted for just 27% of Americans in poverty. White families made up 17% of the poor depicted in news media, but made up 66% of the American poor, the study said.[3]

Many White Americans have found it offensive to consider that people of color are entitled to the same access, competence, and success that they enjoy. Resistance to this kind of racial equality has taken many forms. For example, in 1917, White people in East St. Louis, Illinois, became enraged that Black people were hired to work at factories holding government contracts. During the summer of that year, enraged White citizens committed random acts of racially motivated violence in that city. Between 40 and 250 Black people were murdered and about 6,000 were left homeless; property loss was estimated at $400,000. This tragedy is known as the "East St. Louis Race Massacre."[4]

Before 2016, all of the valedictorians at Cleveland High School in Cleveland, Mississippi, had been White students. In 2016, however, an African American student, Jasmine Shepherd, emerged as the student with the highest grade point average in the graduating class. Despite this fact, she was forced to share this honor with a White co-valedictorian whose GPA was lower. Shepherd sued but lost. In 2019, a federal judge confirmed that the school acted erroneously, but ruled that there was no federal civil rights violation in the school's action.[5]

Sometimes, White Americans who encounter successful people of color find comfort in thinking that these people are the exception, not the rule. When I was at Valparaiso, I heard my White peers often say to me, "You're not like other Black people." While this may have been intended as some sort of indirect compliment, I actually found this to be quite insulting. They'd tell me this, sometimes admitting in the same conversation that I was the only African American they'd ever actually met. This could only mean that the "other Black people" to which I was compared were those that they imagined.

During the summer of my junior year in college, I decided to stay on campus to take classes. I needed a place to stay and a roommate to cut expenses, and I found someone who was willing to share an apartment with me. Kelly, a White student, was an education major. She struck me as one of the most open-minded and progressive people that I'd met at Valpo, and during that summer, we had many meaningful conversations and became good friends.

Still, soon after meeting me, she noted: "You're not like other Black people." When I asked her to elaborate, it became clear that I was only about the second African American that she had ever personally encountered in her life. All of the "other Black people" were figments of her imagination, composites of the stereotypes and factoids about Black people that she had come to know from what she'd seen on television or read in magazines, books, or in the paper (there was no internet back then).

I was always amused whenever White peers assumed me to somehow be different from other Black people. That summer, Kelly and I had ample time for probing, honest, and transparent conversations. I was happy to explain to her that, where I came from, there were quite a few more Black people who were far superior to me in talent, intelligence, and achievement. West Side High School in Gary, Indiana, was full of high achievers, nearly all of whom were people of color. Among West Side's alumni are doctors, attorneys, entrepreneurs, artists, professional athletes, educators, and engineers, some nationally (or internationally) prominent. As I reflect on my life from my current vantage point, I can confirm that my peers from West Side High School were among the most gifted cohort of people I'd ever meet. Their stories inspire me.

By the end of that summer, Kelly came to understand that I was, indeed, like many, many other Black people. She became comfortable with the idea that Black people are often highly driven to achieve success and meaning in their lives, not just for themselves, but for their families and communities. She also came to understand that our skin color makes us vulnerable in ways that she would never experience. In turn, I came to understand that Kelly's questions were genuine and legitimate. Her ignorance was of neither her creation nor her choosing; she was disadvantaged by the wall of privilege that encased her.

I don't remember which classes I took that summer. Even if I could recall the classes, it is unlikely that I would remember any of the lectures or readings. The most enduring lessons were the ones that Kelly and I learned from each other. Over cold pizza and wine coolers, we had conversations about race that were probing and authentic— conversations that converted us from roommates to genuine friends.

15

Am I a Racist if I Don't
Want My Taxes to
Provide Welfare for
People Who Won't
Work?

The Short Answer

The assumption that Black Americans utilize more public assistance dollars than other groups is inaccurate. In reality, White Americans utilize more public assistance dollars than any other group.[1] Despite this fact, the stereotype that people of color abuse welfare persists.

The stereotype of the Black "Welfare Queen" may be rooted, in large part, in the 1976 presidential campaign of Ronald Reagan. In his widely publicized campaign speeches, he made frequent anecdotal reference to a Chicago woman who had a notorious record for abusing the welfare system. Writer Josh Levin notes that this woman, who became commonly known as "the Welfare Queen," was held up by Reagan as evidence of a system rife with openings for fraud and abuse by people too lazy to work. Levin notes, however, that this woman, one of whose 33 known aliases was "Linda Taylor," did not represent the average Chicago welfare recipient. She was an exception, an extreme con artist whose numerous crimes included not only welfare fraud, but an extensive record of other offenses including social security fraud, veterans' benefits fraud, suspected kidnapping, and even murder. In choosing Linda Taylor as his evidence that welfare recipients routinely abuse the system, he placed an unfortunate and unfair stigma upon the numerous honest people with legitimate needs for assistance.[2] Although her race may have been assumed in the public's imagination, it is not entirely clear that the "Welfare Queen" was a Black woman. Writing for *National Public Radio*, Gene Denby noted:

> Taylor's own racial reality is much harder to pin down. . . . Born Martha Miller, she was listed as White in the 1930 Census, just like everyone else in her family. But she had darker skin and darker hair. People who knew her family told Levin that she had Native American ancestry. One of her husbands, who was Black, said she could look like an Asian woman at times. Another earlier husband and ostensible father to some of her children was White, and during that marriage she gave birth to kids who alternately appeared Black, unmistakably White, or racially ambiguous. At times she posed as a Jewish woman. In one photo, she has long, blonde hair.[3]

More to Consider

Despite Ronald Reagan's unfair stigmatization of public assistance recipients, there is no evidence of any correlation between the need for aid and the lack of a work ethic. In fact, people who live at or beneath the poverty line are often the hardest working people in this country.

For many honest and hardworking people, the fact is that poverty often perpetuates poverty. Here are two examples that illustrate this: When I was in graduate school, I met a woman who was seeking services for her daughter at the psychologist's office where I worked. The woman's daughter had a learning disability. In order to get assistance for her daughter, however, she needed a psychologist to administer a test in order to diagnose and certify the condition. A single mother with two children (one of whom was the daughter in question), she took time off from her job and caught the bus to get to the doctor's office for the required test. Because of the undependable bus schedule and the walk with two young children from the bus stop to the office, however, she arrived to her appointment 25 minutes late. As the receptionist, I greeted her, but was forced to ask her to reschedule. I was heartbroken as she explained that requesting more time off from work would cause her to get fired from her job. So this woman, who happened to be African American, faced the possible loss of her job in order to care for her daughter, thus placing her in possible legitimate need of public assistance. Too often, poverty reinforces poverty.

While I lived in Tulsa, I came to know of a woman, a young mother, who was in jail because she could not afford to pay the $300 needed to settle an overdue ticket. Overdue library books, parking tickets, and late fees are not the offenses of hardened criminals; they are minor offenses of which many have been guilty from time to time, regardless of race or socio-economic status. For this woman, however, the original $50 fine was too burdensome to bear; once the fine ballooned to $300, the amount was well beyond her means. So she was sentenced to several months in jail, separated from her young children who were then forced to be without her care and left vulnerable without her protection. Having been arrested and jailed, the young woman would have a difficult time finding work to support her family once released. Fortunately, I was part of an organization that paid her $300 fine so that she could be released in time to spend Christmas with her children. What we could not do, however, was erase the permanent stain of a criminal record from this young woman's life although her only crime was that she was poor.

Most people are more than willing to work hard to care for themselves and their families. Reliance on public assistance is not an aspiration, but a necessity. Too often, however, racial stereotypes present barriers to opportunities for employment. A 2003 study published in the *American Journal of Sociology* found that a White man with a criminal record is more likely to get hired than a Black man whose record is clean.[4] This shows that, despite the qualifications of the applicant, race alone may impact the hiring preferences of employers.

16

Isn't Affirmative Action Racist Because It Gives Preference Based Upon Race?

The Short Answer

In 2008, Abigail Fisher, a White woman, filed a lawsuit against the University of Texas at Austin. Her lawsuit claimed that she was denied admission to the university because less-qualified Black and Hispanic students were admitted instead. Her right to equal protection under the law, she alleged, had thus been violated. The case remained in litigation for several years. In 2013, the Supreme Court sent the case back to the lower courts for reevaluation. Finally, in June of 2016, the Supreme Court ruled 4 to 3 in favor of the University, citing the lawfulness of its "race conscious" admissions program.[1]

Colleges around the country were attuned to the case, as its outcome would potentially have far-reaching implications for collegiate admissions practices throughout America. The Fisher case also gave voice to a very real fear emerging among some White people, one that was present but remained largely unspoken in polite circles: Wasn't the consideration of race in college admissions just the flip side of the nasty practice of considering race at all? By privileging minorities, weren't White people in danger of losing opportunities that were rightfully theirs?

Affirmative Action was originally intended to correct decades-old inequities by assuring opportunities to those who had long been denied them on the basis of race or gender. Imagine that you dream of becoming a doctor. You finish high school with honors. You earn a competitive scholarship to a good college and graduate with your degree in biology with honors. You take the MCAT, the entrance exam for medical school, and you score in the top 5% of all the applicants. Despite your achievements and qualifications, however, no medical school will accept you simply because you are a Black person. Meanwhile, White applicants with lower grades and MCAT scores are routinely admitted to medical school. They graduate and become doctors, and they leave to their children and their children's children financial security, social stability, and a lifestyle full of comforts, privileges, and opportunities.

Because you are a Black person, despite your credentials, your effort to pursue your dream meets with a dead end. You spend your entire working life as a lab assistant. Because you were barred from becoming a doctor on the basis of your race, you leave to your children and your children's children considerably less in the way of financial security, social stability, and overall opportunity.

Affirmative Action was initiated by the Kennedy administration in 1961 and extended by the Johnson administration. The intent of the policy was to level the historically unlevel playing field by ensuring the flow of employment and educational opportunities to those who were historically denied those opportunities because of their race or gender. Affirmative Action, therefore, is not unfair; it is corrective.

More to Consider

An unintended consequence of Affirmative Action is that it can sometimes stigmatize women and people of color by calling into question the validity of their qualifications. For some, it may reinforce the unfounded belief that only White men are truly capable of advancing on their own merit, while less-prepared women and people of color can only get ahead if afforded this unfair advantage. Two incidents from my own career underscore this point. When I was hired as an assistant professor, I was the only African American person on the faculty in my department. Shortly after my hire, a colleague, a White man, came to my office to introduce himself. After initial greetings and some polite conversation, he ended his visit by stating, "At first I was worried that you were one of those Affirmative Action hires. But I've reviewed your credentials; since your degree is from Indiana University, I guess you're okay."

Clearly, the purpose of his visit to my office was not to welcome or befriend me, but to put me on notice. He wanted me to know that he found me to be suspect, an imposter, perhaps, and that my degree from an institution of which he approved checked off one of the ways that I'd need to prove to him my worthiness to be there.

Within a year of that incident, another colleague, a White man (who happened also to be one of my former professors), came to my office, clearly disturbed. I knew that he was up for tenure and that it was a stressful time for him. But I was unprepared for what he was about to say to me. "Teresa, you know that I like you. But your being here does not bode well for me." With that, he gave me a hug and left.

Your being here does not bode well for me. That statement, coupled with the very awkward hug, was an expression of the conflict that he felt at both knowing me as a person (by that time, for eight years as both his former grad student and his new, young colleague), and seeing me as a Black woman. At this very stressful time in his life, it was my gender and my race that threatened him. Specifically, he felt threatened by my Black, female presence in a profession historically dominated by White men.

All people wish to be regarded for their achievements, their qualifications, and their strength of character. No one wants the stigma of dubious merit, and no one wants to live in a state of heightened anxiety that comes with the constant need to prove your worth beyond the credentials you've already earned. While this is the "tax" that many women and Black professionals pay, we also realize that, without Affirmative Action, many of us with doctorate degrees might be locked out of the careers we've sought.

17

Why Don't Black People Accept and Welcome Me When I Try to Interact With Them?

The Short Answer

There could be many reasons for this. In my experience, I have never known African American people to reject or exclude White people simply because they are White. Black people have a tendency to embrace anyone and everyone who exhibits authenticity. There may be times, however, that we express displeasure with people who we perceive to be presumptuous, condescending, or disrespectful.

More to Consider

Families have certain proprietary relational rights. Imagine your family around the dinner table having conversations that are unique to your close relationship. In the space of your family time, you feel comfortable discussing shared history, sensitive matters, personal problems, family secrets, and private jokes. Imagine how uncomfortable you'd feel if a coworker dropped in uninvited and unannounced, pulled up a seat to your table, and joined in the conversation. Even if the coworker appeared with a box of chocolates and an expensive bottle of wine, nothing would dispel the sense that his presence was presumptuous, disruptive, and awkward.

Fraternities and sororities are very similar in that they have clearly defined boundaries, separating those within their circles from those outside of them. Members of these organizations are bound together by experiences, rituals, missions, memories, and legacies that create for them a unique, shared identity. Imagine the reaction that a non-member would get upon dropping in on a fraternity or sorority meeting uninvited.

Despite the great diversity within and across our various Black communities, African American people have what might be described as a connection that is loosely akin to a family bond. I have found this to be the case in my travels and experiences around the United States and the world. Whether in Gary, Indiana, or in Tulsa, Oklahoma, or in Dakar, Senegal, or in Port of Spain, Trinidad, or in Kingston, Jamaica, or Louisville, Kentucky, my experience has been that of an acknowledged kinship with others of African descent. Our shared history and experiences, and the common elements of our cultures make our interactions with each other meaningful in a unique way, even if we are strangers meeting for the first time. This is why, in an integrated setting, the Black people will often quickly find each other and naturally form their own group.

I have seen White people, with good intentions, attempt to insert themselves into situations and conversations where a group of African American people are clearly communing with each other in a particularly "familial" way. Rather than ask to join, they simply show up—much like the coworker who drops in unannounced during your family dinner. If you received a lukewarm welcome in a scenario like this, you were likely giving the impression that you assumed you had a right to be included, whether or not you were actually invited to join at that particular moment. Your assumption may have come from the privilege you have always enjoyed as a White person; one element of that privilege is the presumption of access to everything.

If the scenario described here sounds familiar, and you believe that you have been unwelcome in Black circles, don't give up. More than likely, that same group of African American people would be delighted to welcome, befriend, and embrace you if you use a slightly different approach. Try it again. Only this time, respectfully request to be included, holding space for the possibility that your request may be denied. And when you are included, seek authentic friendship by listening, learning, and respecting the right of the "family" to retreat occasionally to its own space.

18

Why Can't Black People Forget About Slavery, Let Go of the Past, and Move On?

The Short Answer

From earliest American Colonial times, there was a recognition that slavery was both wrong and a direct contradiction to the ideals of liberty and equality. Among the founding fathers, the slavery debate underscored the tension between moral consciousness and economic prosperity. An early draft of the *Declaration of Independence* includes Thomas Jefferson's condemnation of King George for fostering the slave trade, which he called "a cruel war against human nature." This passage, however, was removed from the final draft of the *Declaration*. And Jefferson himself was a participant in this "cruel war against human nature." He owned more than 200 enslaved Black people. The other 11 American presidents who owned enslaved Black people included George Washington, James Madison, James Monroe, Andrew Jackson, Martin Van Buren, William Henry Harrison, John Tyler, James K. Polk, Zachary Taylor, Andrew Johnson, and Ulysses S. Grant.[1]

The Thirteenth Amendment abolished American slavery in 1865. The practices, customs, and power structure of slavery, however, extended well into the 20th century. Vestiges of slavery persist today. Most African American surnames are the ones given to an enslaved ancestor by the White person who owned him or her. My family name, "Shelton," comes to me by way of slavery because someone in my ancestral line was owned by someone whose last name was Shelton. While my ancestor who was transported to America was an African with his own African name, customs, religion, and memories, the English/Irish slave name "Shelton" was imposed upon this African person (or upon that person's descendent) upon enslavement. This renaming forever supplanted the name that was given to him at birth, the name that linked my ancestor to his family, his origin, and his true identity.

Slavery thus makes it very difficult, if not impossible, for me and for most African American people to trace ancestry back much further than great-grandparents. Enslaved families were split up and surnames of the enslaved changed with changes in ownership. (Therefore, my ancestor could have been Henry McKinley as a child, Henry Williams as a teenager, Henry Mitchell as a young adult, and Henry Shelton at the time of Emancipation.) The enslaved were born and buried with records that were vague at best and nonexistent at worst, leaving almost nothing of a paper trail for posterity to investigate. Owners of enslaved people were intentional about erasing the personal identities of their captives, and that loss of genealogy is passed to me.

Along with the surnames of most African American people, the present-day names of highways, bridges, monuments, and historical icons are contemporary reminders of slavery. I live in Louisville, Kentucky. Kentucky was a slave state, and I encounter reminders of slavery almost every time I leave my home for business, work, or recreation. The land within a mile of my current home was once plantation property where enslaved people lived and worked.[2] Nearly every day, I drive past the well-preserved plantation home on Shelbyville Road which was constructed in 1843 and originally occupied by its White owners and the enslaved Black people who served them. Shelbyville Road is itself named in honor of Isaac Shelby (1750-1826), Kentucky's first governor, who, like many of the elite of his day, owned enslaved people.

Whenever I head west to the U of L campus on Interstate 64, I pass the exit to Breckinridge Lane, which is named for the family of the same name. John Breckinridge was a Virginia enslaver and the patriarch of the Kentucky Breckinridge family. In 1792, he marched 18 of his enslaved people on foot from Virginia to Kentucky along the route that is present-day I-64 in order to rent these human beings out for profit.[3]

Like colleges and universities that owe their existence to the unpaid labor of enslaved Africans, many modern-day corporations have begun to acknowledge the connection between their current fortunes and slavery. Some of these corporations include Lehman Brothers, Aetna Insurance, JP Morgan Chase, New York Life, Wachovia Corporation, Norfolk Southern Railroad, and others.[4] JP Morgan Chase issued the following in a statement in January 2005:

> Today, we are reporting that this research found that, between 1831 and 1865, two of our

predecessor banks—Citizens Bank and Canal Bank in Louisiana—accepted approximately 13,000 enslaved individuals as collateral on loans and took ownership of approximately 1,250 of them when the plantation owners defaulted on the loans.[5]

Religious entities have also endorsed and profited from slavery. The Catholic Church, at various times, was the largest corporate owner of enslaved people in Florida, Louisiana, Maryland, Kentucky, and Missouri.[6] The Southern Baptist Convention was founded in 1845 when it split from Northern Baptists over the issue of slavery, which it supported. In 1995, the SBC issued a formal apology for its support of slavery and its history of segregation. In 2017, it formally condemned White supremacists.[7]

These and other vestiges of slavery are 21st-century reminders that millions of our ancestors spent their lives serving and enriching others without ever receiving compensation for themselves and their own posterity. The wealth gap that exists today between White people and African American people ties directly to slavery.

Therefore, while slavery legally ended with the Thirteenth Amendment, its impact remains. Furthermore, the enormous debt owed to enslaved Africans and their descendants has never been settled. African American people continue to seek equality in a country that the free labor of their ancestors helped build.

More to Consider

Present-day African American people also suffer from the inherited psychological trauma of slavery and the harmful impact of Jim Crow segregation. It is only recently, however, that the field of psychology has begun to research and discuss this issue. In 2013, for example, *Contemporary Family Therapy* published an article titled "Residual Effects of Slavery: What Clinicians Need to Know."[8] In describing RES (Residual Effects of Slavery) as a unique kind of trauma, the authors state:

> It is important to note that African Americans, like other ethnic groups, are diverse, and reactions to RES vary. Regardless, the literature suggests that RES can affect multiple generations because direct exposure to the trauma is not necessary for individuals and families to feel its effects . . . . The trauma associated with slavery is unique because it has yet to be accepted as having had profound implications. Theorists have attempted to explicate the ways in which African Americans have adopted behaviors in response to the

viciousness of slavery and its after effects. Newly liberated African Americans did not receive mental health care for probable PTSD following the abolition of slavery. . . Instead of treating the trauma of slavery with healing centers, newly freed African Americans were raped, castrated, and lynched . . . . Post-Traumatic Slave Syndrome has been used to explain the multigenerational transmission of trauma, which includes behaviors associated with lowered self-esteem, anger, and feelings of inferiority.[9]

The authors further associate "Post-Traumatic Slave Syndrome" with "the persistent presence of racism, despite the significant legal, social, and political progress made during the last half of the twentieth century," noting that it "has created a physiological risk for Black people that is virtually unknown to White Americans . . . .".[10]

19

Why Is There So Much Attention to Black Lives Matter?

The Short Answer

The preceding chapters provide the answer to this question. In America, it is a fact that those people with darker skin access fewer opportunities and face greater risks than those people who are White. Those with darker skin are judged more harshly and are punished more severely than White counterparts who commit the same offenses. Those with darker skin also endure the stress of spending their mental resources to challenge the stereotypes, falsehoods, and negative assumptions that society holds about them. People with darker skin are often assumed to be guilty until proven innocent, while White people are often assumed to be innocent until proven guilty.

April 19, 1995, started as a normal day in Oklahoma City. People there awakened to their alarm clocks, brewed their morning coffee, and had breakfast. By 8:00 a.m., the flow of morning rush-hour traffic was well underway as kids headed to school and adults headed to their various workplaces. There was the unremarkable normalcy of a beautiful, spring Wednesday morning.

And then, at 9:02 a.m., a bomb exploded.

On that day, I was living in Tulsa (a short drive from Oklahoma City). I had stopped into a Walmart and happened to pass by the electronics department, where the display of multiple television sets featured on their screens the same breaking news story. The black billowing smoke and debris seemed, at first, to be the scene of war. This, however, was no foreign battlefield. This was the Alfred P. Murrah Federal Building, just two hours away from where I stood, and directly across the street from where my fiance's aunt lived. The death toll was 168, with another 680 injured, and property damage for miles around. The earliest reports were that this was possibly the work of a Middle Eastern terrorist.

That same day, an Oklahoma state trooper noticed a yellow Mercury on Interstate 35 without a registration tag. When the trooper pulled the driver over, he noticed the outline of a weapon on his person. The driver was carrying both a loaded .45 caliber Glock and a knife. The trooper placed handcuffs on the driver, peacefully took him into custody, and delivered him to jail. It turns out that the driver was Timothy McVeigh, who was later convicted and executed for the 168 lives lost in the Oklahoma City Bombing.[1]

On July 6, 2016, Philando Castile was stopped by police at around 9:00 p.m. while driving with his partner and their young daughter in a suburb of St. Paul, Minnesota. When the officer asked Castile for his license and registration, Castile proceeded to comply, informing the officer in that moment that he had a firearm, which he was licensed to carry. When Castile reached for his license and registration, the officer shot him seven times at close range. By 9:37 p.m., Castile was pronounced dead.[2]

Had McVeigh been a Black man, one wonders whether he would have survived the traffic stop that day in Oklahoma

City on I-35. Had Castile been a White man, one wonders whether he would still be alive.

More to Consider

We say that Black lives matter because they do. Every unarmed African American person whose life was erased in a reactionary moment of weak judgement was someone's brother, son, nephew, father, husband, sister, mother, daughter, niece, wife, or friend. These lives lost are empty seats at dinner tables, absent mothers and fathers at graduations, weddings, and baby showers; absent loved ones at Thanksgiving, Christmas, Kwanzaa, and Juneteenth celebrations. They are voices absent from choirs and hugs absent at bedtime. Every one of these is someone who was cherished, someone who is now sorely missed, someone whose memory lingers in the air. These lives lost are ones that might have been spared had they been White people— White people like Timothy McVeigh.

With each such tragedy reported in the news, African American people grieve anew. Here is a representative list of some of those we grieve—unarmed African American people—many of whose stories have been widely reported. You can search the internet to learn more about them.[3] Sadly, this list is far from comprehensive. It could extend for hundreds of pages and for centuries into the past.

Daunte Wright, 2000-2021

George Perry Floyd, 1973-2020

Dreasjon "Sean" Reed, 1999-2020

Michael Brent Charles Ramos, 1978-2020

Breonna Taylor, 1993-2020

Manuel "Mannie" Elijah Ellis, 1986-2020

Atatiana Koquice Jefferson, 1990-2019

Emantic "EJ" Fitzgerald Bradford Jr., 1997-2018

Charles "Chop" Roundtree Jr., 2000-2018

Chinedu Okobi, 1982-2018

Botham Shem Jean, 1991-2018

Antwon Rose Jr., 2000-2018

Saheed Vassell, 1983-2018

Stephon Alonzo Clark, 1995-2018

Aaron Bailey, 1972-2017

Charleena Chavon Lyles, 1987-2017

Fetus of Charleena Chavon Lyles, 2017

Jordan Edwards, 2001-2017

Chad Robertson, 1992-2017

Deborah Danner, 1950-2016

Alfred Olango, 1978-2016

Terence Crutcher, 1976-2016

Terrence LeDell Sterling, 1985-2016

Korryn Gaines, 1993-2016

Joseph Curtis Mann, 1966-2016

Philando Castile, 1983-2016

Alton Sterling, 1979-2016

Bettie "Betty Boo" Jones, 1960-2015

Quintonio LeGrier, 1996-2015

Corey Lamar Jones, 1984-2015

Jamar O'Neal Clark, 1991-2015

Jeremy "Bam Bam" McDole, 1987-2015

India Kager, 1988-2015

Samuel Vincent DuBose, 1972-2015

Sandra Bland, 1987-2015

Brendon K. Glenn, 1986-2015

Freddie Carlos Gray Jr., 1989-2015

Walter Lamar Scott, 1965-2015

Eric Courtney Harris, 1971-2015

Phillip Gregory White, 1982-2015

Mya Shawatza Hall, 1987-2015

Meagan Hockaday, 1988-2015

Tony Terrell Robinson, Jr., 1995-2015

Janisha Fonville, 1994-2015

Natasha McKenna, 1978-2015

Jerame C. Reid, 1978-2014

Rumain Brisbon, 1980-2014

Tamir Rice, 2002-2014

Akai Kareem Gurley, 1986-2014

Tanisha N. Anderson, 1977-2014

Dante Parker, 1977-2014

Ezell Ford, 1988-2014

Michael Brown Jr., 1996-2014

John Crawford III, 1992-2014

Eric Garner, 1970-2014

Dontre Hamilton, 1983-2014

Victor White III, 1991-2014

Gabriella Monique Nevarez, 1991-2014

Yvette Smith, 1966-2014

McKenzie J. Cochran, 1988-2014

Jordan Baker, 1988-2014

Andy Lopez, 2000-2013

Miriam Iris Carey, 1979-2013

Barrington "BJ" Williams, 1988-2013

Jonathan Ferrell, 1989-2013

Carlos Alcis, 1970- 2013

Larry Eugene Jackson Jr., 1980-2013

Kyam Livingston, 1975-2013

Clinton R. Allen, 1987-2013

Kimani "KiKi" Gray, 1996-2013

Kayla Moore, 1971-2013

Jamaal Moore Sr., 1989-2012

Johnnie Kamahi Warren, 1968-2012

Shelly Marie Frey, 1985-2012

Darnisha Diana Harris, 1996-2012

Timothy Russell, 1968-2012

Malissa Williams, 1982-2012

Noel Palanco, 1989-2012

Reynaldo Cuevas, 1992-2012

Chavis Carter, 1991-2012

Alesia Thomas, 1977-2012

Shantel Davis, 1989-2012

Sharmel T. Edwards, 1962-2012

Tamon Robinson, 1985-2012

Ervin Lee Jefferson, III, 1994-2012

Kendrec McDade, 1992-2012

Rekia Boyd, 1989-2012

Shereese Francis, 1982-2012

Jersey K. Green, 1974-2012

Wendell James Allen, 1991-2012

Nehemiah Lazar Dillard, 1982-2012

Dante' Lamar Price, 1986-2012

Raymond Luther Allen Jr., 1978-2012

Trayvon Martin, 1995-2012

Manual Levi Loggins Jr., 1980-2012

Ramarley Graham, 1993-2012

Kenneth Chamberlain Sr., 1943-2011

Alonzo Ashley Jr., 1982-2011

Kenneth Harding Jr., 1991-2011

Derek Williams, 1989-2011

Raheim Brown, Jr., 1990-2011

Reginald Doucet, 1985-2011

Derrick Jones, 1973-2010

Danroy "DJ" Henry Jr., 1990-2010

Aiyana Mo'Nay Stanley-Jones, 2002-2010

Steven Eugene Washington, 1982-2010

Aaron Campbell, 1984-2010

20

As a White American, How Can I Respond Effectively to Racial Injustice?

The Short Answer

You can do plenty. As a White American, you were born with privilege and access that people of color simply do not have in the same way. Therefore, you have more power than you may realize to make positive change. By reading this book, you've already taken an important step. Clearly, you have an open mind and a desire to treat others as you would wish to be treated. None of us can go back and change the past, but we can certainly make huge strides toward bringing justice into our present and our future. We can co-create an America where diversity is embraced and equity, inclusion, and justice prevail.

- Become as informed as you can about African American people and other people of color. While there are many good books you can read and great documentaries and films you can view, your most important knowledge will come from interacting with people who are different than you. Interacting respectfully and intentionally with people of color will better equip you to see life through their lens. In the process, authentic friendships may develop.

- Become sensitized to racial bias, and don't tolerate it. In your own family and social circles, take notice of racist comments and jokes. Don't be complicit in "fun" that dehumanizes anyone on the basis of race, gender,

gender identity, sexual orientation, class, national origin, or other factors that may mark difference. When they occur, turn those awkward situations into teaching moments. Use statements like, "I know that was meant to be funny, but how would you feel if you were a Black person and that joke was being told about you?"

- Become an ally in the way that is most comfortable to you. In the wake of the Breonna Taylor and George Floyd murders, millions of people of all races, ages, and creeds took to the streets to protest. It was encouraging and uplifting for African American people that so many joined in with the cry for justice. This type of participation, however, is not for everyone. If you wish to become an ally in a less conspicuous way, that is perfectly fine. Writing a letter to a senator to challenge a racist position, or simply befriending those who appear marginalized can be equally powerful gestures of activism as carrying a sign in a public march.

- When racial tragedy is in the news, don't retreat to your safety zone. Instead, opt to reach out to the African American people in your circle because they are hurting. Each instance of tragedy brings more trauma and threatens to add more layers of distrust that keep people apart. Your intentional presence can bring healing. If you find yourself struggling with what to say, try these words:

"I can't know exactly what you are feeling because I'm not in your shoes. But I am standing with you. I know your pain is deep and real. I am so sorry. I am right here."

- If you are serious about developing authentic friendships with people of color, prepare yourself to deal with occasional feelings of discomfort as you learn more about the historical trauma that lies at the root of present-day unrest. Resist the temptation to become paralyzed by feelings of guilt or hopelessness. Instead, understand and embrace this as part of your particular struggle, and commit to seeing it through. Stay engaged. Stay at the table. Have the courage to embrace honest conversations whenever they come up; and see that courage as your part of healing the world.

- Join a group of White people who are committed to learning about race. Work with them to understand how being White has impacted your view and your experience of the world. A good example of such a group is the one at All Souls Unitarian Church in Tulsa, Oklahoma. This church hosts robust programming to help White people educate themselves on race. Their group, REWIRE, meets regularly to help White people unlearn racism, and it has expanded to other nonprofits and states beyond Oklahoma. (More information can be found at rewireglobal.org, and more about the church's programming is found at http://allsoulschurch.org/ programs/ #intercultural-work.)

More to Consider

At the beginning of this book, I defined *racist* as a person who has resolved that a human being's worth is based upon the color of their skin. Racists believe, for example, that White people are inherently superior by virtue of their Whiteness, and that people of color are inherently inferior because they are not White. If you were inclined at all to read this book, you are likely not a racist according to this definition. For even the most hardened of racists, however, there is hope. When ignorance melts, fear goes away, and even the stoniest of hearts can change.

In 1971, civil rights activist Ann Atwater and former KKK member C.P. Ellis became lifelong friends after co-chairing a series of contentious meetings to address school desegregation in Durham, North Carolina. Their presumably unlikely friendship was documented in the 1996 book and subsequent 2019 film *The Best of Enemies*.[1] U.S. Senator Robert Byrd of West Virginia served in Congress for 52 years and died in 2010. A former member and organizer of the KKK, he endorsed Obama in 2008.[2] Arno Michaelis, founding member of a worldwide racist skinhead organization, is now a motivational speaker who advocates for racial diversity and unity. He is the author of *My Life After Hate* (2010).[3] These and many other examples are proof that even the most ardent of racists have the capacity to change.

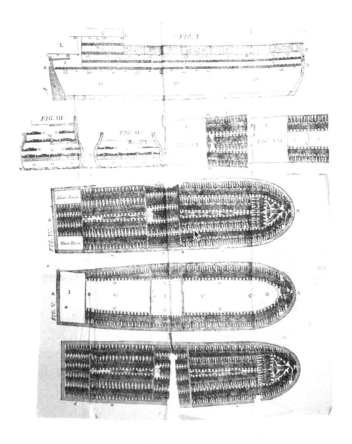

This is a diagram of a slave ship which illustrates the packing of human beings as cargo to be transported from West Africa and sold in the Caribbean and in Colonial America/the United States of America. Millions of Africans arrived in the United States and in the Caribbean aboard a slave ship in this way.

(This document is dated 1814. Source: Creative Commons. In the public domain.)

African American enslaved people had no agency when it came to their own families and children. Yet, they were commonly charged with the care and rearing of White children. This type of image, showing a Black servant holding a White child, was very common during the late 1800s.

(This photo is circa 1860. Source: Creative Commons. In the public domain.)

This African American family is pictured on a southern plantation in the early 1900s. Although slavery was abolished decades earlier, the family's living and working conditions are virtually identical to what enslaved persons experienced. Barriers to opportunities in education, voting, and financial security trapped many African American people in poverty long after slavery ended.

(This photo is circa 1900. Source: Creative Commons. In the public domain.)

Once slavery ended, many southern towns established vagrancy laws that made it easy to arrest and sentence Black men to hard labor. In this way, the South was able to recover some of the free labor that disappeared once slavery was abolished. Many of these African American chain gang laborers likely received prison sentences for the "crime" of being without homes or jobs.

(This photo is circa 1920. Source: Creative Commons. In the public domain.)

Enslaved African Americans were commonly forbidden to learn to read and write. Nonetheless, some did learn at both their own peril and the peril of those who dared to teach them. Black people enthusiastically pursued education when it was legal to do so. Black schools, however, typically had few resources, and those in the southern states were vulnerable to Klan terror. More than 40 Muskogee, Oklahoma children are pictured in this photo taken in 1917. It would have been common for a single teacher, working in a one-room school, to instruct this many children or more.

(This photo is dated 1917. Source: Creative Commons. In the public domain.)

For about a full century after the end of slavery, racial segregation was the legally enforced norm, particularly in the South. Racial inequality was held in place for generations by a custom of strict separation of the races in everything from business to entertainment. These artifacts and images are from that era.

(These photos were taken in the 1950s/1960s. Source: Creative Commons. All are in the public domain.)

This photo from the 1963 March on Washington shows some of the thousands who gathered from around the United States to demand equality for Black Americans in jobs, education, voting, and housing.

(This photo is dated 1963. Source: Creative Commons.
In the public domain.)

Sybrina Fulton and Tracy Martin, parents of Trayvon Martin, attending one of the many   protests that followed their son's February 26, 2012, murder at the hands of George Zimmerman.

(Source: Creative Commons. In the public domain.)

Let

the

Healing

Begin

21

We Are Family
(Dysfunctional Perhaps,
but Family Nonetheless)

The narrative about race and racial difference in this country is dominated by a paradigm of opposition—White people opposed to Black people, Black people opposed to White people, White people opposed to Affirmative Action, and Black people opposed to discrimination. Even the nicknames for our racial identifiers—"Black" and "White"—presuppose two realities that are as opposite as possible. I say that I'm a Black person, but my skin is some brown shade between honey and mocha; and in my Black family are all the shades of brown from lightest beige to deepest coffee. The people I call White do not look the shade of paper from my printer or the color of whole milk. Instead, I find White people to be various shades of ivory, tan, and pink. Despite having little resemblance to the literal colors *white* and *black*, the fact that we are content to describe ourselves with these particular words makes a powerful statement about the undeniable way that contrast frames our racial reality.

Viewing our racial dynamic in black-and-white terms (pun intended) leaves little space to address racial realities that don't fit neatly into clear-cut categories. There is no question in my mind that Black people and White people don't experience American life in the same way. What truths remain about us if we delete *different* from the list of adjectives that summarize our relationship to one another? We may well discover that *difference* is not the entire story of who we are.

Much of what I know about race and racial difference in America comes from my own experience of being in the minority. I make no claim whatsoever to speak for all African American people, and I expect that many Black people have valid perspectives that contradict what I've presented here. Yet, I've encountered many African American people whose stories include elements that resonate with mine.

For example, in many Black families (mine included), there has been among our elders a custom of intentional amnesia. Many of our foremothers and forefathers perfected the art of erasing with their own silence the experiences about which they didn't want their descendants to know. For the millions of us who descend from the Southern-born African American people who migrated Northward between 1910 and 1940 in search of a better life, the oral history of the family effectively begins in points North. In leaving the brutal, Jim Crow South behind and creating a fresh start for their posterity, these ancestors were determined to shield their children from their own nightmares. And so, their tendency was to go silent, often taking to their graves, not only their own trauma and pain, but the many anomalies and complexities of race and racism that were difficult to categorize and harder to explain. Many of our ancestors never fully shared with us their stories—stories like this one:

Jessie Lee Mahone was born on a quivering fault line in

American history. The year of her birth—1900—was a divider between generations of Black Americans who had lived as enslaved people, and later generations of Black Americans who would have no personal memory of it.

Her father, Dennis Mahone, had been enslaved in Mississippi. At the sunset of the 19th century, Dennis found his way to Prudence Crossing, Alabama. His journey there was risky and treacherous. Because of vagrancy laws throughout the Southern states, Dennis could be accused at any point by any White person who encountered him of the crime of being without work; and this simple accusation could have resulted in his arrest and imprisonment for months, or years, or for the rest of his life. This ever-present danger notwithstanding, Dennis made it across the state line to the eastern edge of Alabama.

There, he met Kitty Griffin, a 40-year-old widow and mother of seven living children. In 1900, Kitty had Jessie Lee, her eighth child and the first of her two children with Dennis. The historical record shows that Kitty and Dennis were legally married on September 14, 1905.

Adjacent to the all-Black community of Prudence Crossing was the town of Pittsview, Alabama. Pittsview you could find on a map; Prudence Crossing, you could not. But it was the real locus for the Black sharecropping community who retreated to their homes there after laboring all day in the cotton fields of the neighboring plantations—the same plantations where many of them, their parents, grandparents, and other ancestors had provided free labor their entire lives.

Jessie Lee spent most of her childhood working in the cotton fields alongside her siblings and parents. It was the work that everyone in her community did, and for most Black people in Alabama, it was the only future possible to realistically imagine. And although her fingers bled from the sharp edges of the boll and the mosquitos feasted on her skin during the long hours in the humid heat of the scorching sun, at least she got to spend every day, all day, with the siblings, parents, and extended family who loved her.

It was back-breaking work. Because of the egregiously low pay for picking cotton (about 4 cents per pound), everyone in the family—from youngsters to elders—had to pitch in. Their combined income enabled the family to survive.

The togetherness of the family was cherished above all else. Jessie Lee's parents and grandparents, having lived through slavery, saw loved ones sold apart from each other. Husbands and wives were sent in opposite directions to distant plantations, and siblings were split up leaving no clue as to where they had gone. The fractured families and the loved ones never seen or heard from again left a gaping hole in the hearts of her elders that refused to heal. The toil itself they despised, but the family's connection was treasured. As they filled their sacks with cotton, Jessie Lee learned the songs, stories, and lessons of her people—lessons meant not for amusement or for entertainment but meant to keep her alive.

Like the lesson of Eben Calhoun. The story of Eben Calhoun was a lesson in power and fear. Most of all, to Black people, it was a warning. On April 29, 1907, Eben Calhoun was lynched. African American people had been terrorized by White mobs for decades, and Alabama held a record for its violence. But for Jessie and her family, this tragedy was near their home; Eben Calhoun was lynched right there in Pittsview. In a small community where everyone was known to everyone else, this was no nameless, faceless victim. This was one of their own.[1]

There is no record of what led to the lynching of Eben Calhoun, nor does there need to be in order for the truth of the situation to be imagined. The racial hierarchy of Pittsview in 1907 was virtually identical to the racial hierarchy of that area a century before, precisely because Black people who opposed it—or who even appeared to oppose it—could be erased. No trial. No judge. No jury. Just erased. And erased in the most brutal, grotesque, and macabre manner for all to see, and for those duly warned to tell and retell. He was accosted by a mob. A noose was placed around his neck, and he was suspended from a tree limb, hanging there until his limp and lifeless body dangled in open, gruesome display. Eben Calhoun could have looked a White man in the eye. Or he could've accidentally brushed against the arm of a White woman; or he could have tried to register to vote. In any case, in Alabama in 1907, the punishment for any of these offenses would have been the same. Often, the local law enforcement of the segregated South supported, cheered, and even participated in the lynching of African American people. This kind of terrorism, therefore, occurred often and with impunity.[2]

These were the stories that Jessie Lee heard as a child of elementary-school age. Before she was seven years old, she already knew that White people were powerful. They were to be obeyed and feared. Between 1900 and 1907, there were some 55 lynchings in Alabama, four of them in Lee, Macon, Bullock, and Barbour, counties adjacent to Russell County where Jessie and her family lived.[3] She might have even seen with her own innocent eyes Eben Calhoun's Black body swinging in the southern breeze, and she might have smelled the stench of his rotting flesh. Who knows.

For Black children like Jessie Lee in Alabama in the early 1900s, a life of manual labor was the norm. For girls and young women, domestic work was the typical expectation. Alabama was thoroughly segregated; and Black schools, where they existed, were usually crowded, poorly resourced, and easy targets for Klan terror. The school year was sketchy and sporadic, and always took second place to work on the farm. For many, education was both irrelevant and a waste of time. Yet, at some point and in some way, Jessie

Lee learned to read and write.

There was a depot in Pittsview and a general store nearby. Pullman Porters—the aristocracy of the Black working class of that day—served on the trains that criss-crossed the country. At their various stops, they delivered to Black communities copies of the nation's premiere Black newspaper, the *Chicago Defender*. In sleepy Southern towns like Pittsview, the *Chicago Defender* was radical literature that Black people best not be caught reading. In it were articles about Black opportunity, upward mobility, better wages, and voting rights. The *Defender* was a window into the exciting world of Northern city life, and it beckoned to Black people to drop their ploughs and cotton sacks and head North.

Jessie picked cotton and learned to cook, clean, read, and write; and she watched her older siblings, one by one, leave Alabama for better opportunities in the North. By the time she was a teenager, several of her siblings, and many relatives from Prudence Crossing, had already left the South for Chicago, where life for Black people included no cotton and no lynchings by torch-wielding Southern, White mobs.

As she entered the prime of young womanhood, Jessie's mother, Kitty, now almost 60 years old, was nearing the last phase of her life. Jessie's father, Dennis, died during her teenage years, although the exact year of Dennis's death is unclear. African American people in the segregated South typically had no birth or death certificates, and they commonly began and departed their lives without official record. There were now fewer wage earners in the household. With her father dead and her mother less able to contribute to the family's income, more responsibility fell to Jessie. Cotton was always there, but it was tortuous work that paid a pittance. Jessie needed to get a job.

John Walker Parkman was born in Chattahoochee County, Georgia, on June 19, 1876. His family was neither rich nor poor, but somewhere in between. The Parkman family lived and worked on a farm and they eventually came to own modest property; there is no evidence that they owned enslaved people.

John was a loner. He left his family and moved westward over the state line to nearby Russell County, Alabama, where he worked on a farm and established a general store. In 1918, he was 42 years old and a bachelor. He had never been married and had no children. He needed a housekeeper.

Between the general store and the farm, John Parkman spent nearly his every waking hour at work. Around 1918, John hired 18-year-old Jessie Lee Mahone to cook and keep house for him. And in 1918, she became pregnant with the first of three children they would have together.

At this point, I pause, cringing at the thought of how that first encounter came to be. My gut says it must have been rape. He was a 42-year-old White man who owned perhaps the only general store for miles around. He had power, and money, and the law on his side. He was more than old enough to be her father. She was poor, Black, young, vulnerable, and at his mercy. In the Jim Crow South, a plot like this almost wrote itself. To a man like John Parkman, any Black woman would have been his for the taking. After all, White men had been raping Black women with impunity since colonial times. Cooking, cleaning, and working for him, alone in the home at the back of his general store, Jessie Lee was a sitting duck.

But there are facts that hint at a different truth. John Parkman had nothing to gain by brutalizing the only known companionship in his lonesome life. By hurting her, he only stood to hurt himself. She was the reason that he retired at the end of the day to a clean home, washed laundry, and well-prepared meals. Perhaps more importantly, she was the reason he had something in his life to value beyond his work, and someone to occupy the space in his life where none of his own family were. Had he raped her, he would most certainly have gotten away with it. And even though she had no recourse and no protection from the law, there was the possibility that Jessie would never return to his home again. Given these facts, brutally raping her made no sense.

There are other clues. Jessie Lee gave birth to their first son, John Henry Parkman, on March 7, 1919, and his arrival announced their relationship to the world. Jessie Lee was a very dark-skinned woman with a complexion near the color of Folger's coffee; and her baby boy, by striking contrast, was a copy of his father and as White as they come.

In 1921, Jessie Lee gave birth to their second child, a daughter, named Johnnie Mae. Like her older brother, she had the White complexion and features of her father. By the time Johnnie Mae was a toddler, the four of them were living together as a family in the home at the back of the general store. Three years later, in 1924, Jessie and John had a third child, Willie, who also resembled his father.

No sane woman names her children after her rapist. *John Henry* and *Johnnie Mae*. These were the names that Jessie Lee chose. In the Jim Crow South, White people and Black people could not legally marry. The very naming of her children, therefore, was an act of defiance and a declaration that their relationship was not forced, as so many typically were; their bond was consensual.

In the early 1920s, racial violence was sweeping the country. The South was an increasingly dangerous place for Black people to be. Seven African American people were lynched in Alabama in 1920 alone.[4] And despite the outbreaks of racial violence around the country during the "Red Summer" of 1921, the signs pointing Black people Northward were abundantly clear. African American people by the droves were leaving their sharecropping lives behind, departing the rural South for Northern and Western cities in such great numbers that history records it as the "Great

Migration." In 1926, Jessie's mother, Kitty, died. Jessie Lee and John could not legally marry. Therefore, upon his eventual death, there was nothing of John's that could legally pass to their children, despite the years and the home and family they shared together. With her mother and father both dead and most of her relatives in Chicago or elsewhere, and no possibility of marrying the father of her three children, Jessie Lee had no future in Alabama.

In 1926, with now a fourth child, Katherine, in tow, Jessie Lee headed North to join her relatives who had gone there before. She went first to Chicago, where she lived for several months with relatives. She eventually settled in East Chicago, Indiana, where she lived on the money that John sent to support her and the children, and the earnings from the "Moonshine" liquor she brewed in her kitchen for the thirsty workers from the nearby steel plant. Her four children—three of whom could nearly pass for White people—grew up and attended integrated schools in an area of the city called "New Addition." There were no plantations and there were no lynchings, and there was ample work to be found in the burgeoning steel industry.

Jessie Lee spent her life in East Chicago surrounded by the family that preceded her in migrating northward from Prudence Crossing. In the early 1940s, both of her sons, John Henry and Willie, entered the military and served in World War II. In 1942, Johnnie Mae gave birth to a daughter, Tobi

Lorraine Upshaw.

Meanwhile, John Walker Parkman remained in the South. After the departure of Jessie and his children, he left Russell County to return to Columbus, Georgia. There, he suffered a stroke and spent his last years as an invalid in the home and under the care of his sister. As far as his family knew, John was a lifelong bachelor and had no wife and no children. A teenaged niece who cared for him, Mary Parkman Colman, recalled his last months. His mind was slipping. According to Mary, her Uncle John repeatedly called out for some mysterious person named "Jess." On December 27, 1950, at the age of 74, John Walker Parkman passed away.

As Jessie Lee entered her golden years, the joy of her life was her family, especially her children and great-grandchildren. Her granddaughter, Tobi Lorraine Upshaw, married and had five daughters. In her 70s, Jessie Lee moved from her home into a senior citizens' apartment complex, where Willie, Johnnie Mae, Tobi, and her five daughters came frequently to visit.

I remember my Great-Grandma Jessie vividly. Sometimes I believe I can still smell the scent of her skin, rich and dark, and fragrant with the chewing tobacco in the silver tin "snuff" can she kept at her feet. She had a gold tooth, kept her hair in braids, and she always wore an apron and stockings that were two shades lighter than her skin twisted just above her kneecaps. Her voice echoed down the hall as she joyfully welcomed the five of us whenever we got off the elevator at the 10th floor to come and visit her at her tiny, immaculate apartment. She was bold and loud and loved to cook and sing gospel songs while slapping her knee to keep the rhythm. She sang "I'm Going Home on the Morning Train" with such fervor that it must have meant something too personal to her for us to know. I can still see her eating in the old African way, bringing to her mouth the bits of collard greens and cornbread that she mashed between her thumb and fingers. I can still taste her sweet potato pie, super-moist turkey and dressing, and the tea cakes and ginger snaps that were an ever-present offering to us. She kept a stash of dollar bills, giving one to each of the five of us for good behavior, or just because she was proud that she had them to give.

During one of those visits, when I was around 10 years old, I leaned into Grandma Jessie's shoulder and placed my hand inside of hers. I was struck by the warmth of her touch and veins and scars that were the marks of a long life filled with hard work. I never felt anything from her but overwhelming acceptance and love. And then I asked her:

"Grandma Jessie, why is your skin so dark, and my grandmother's skin so light?"

She paused. The few seconds of silence fell on me like a cold, weighted blanket. There was pain and an unmistakable, unforgettable sternness in her voice. "We won't talk about that," was her succinct response. I knew from her tone that the matter was closed.

In 1980, my mother, my Grandmother Johnnie Mae, and my Uncle Willie gathered near to care for Great-Grandma Jessie, whose health was rapidly failing. In August of 1980, our matriarch passed away. After her death, found among her few possessions was a daguerrotype in pristine condition, an old image of a young White man whose face matched that of my Uncle John Henry, my Grandmother Johnnie Mae, and my Uncle Willie.

After Grandma Jessie left the South, neither she nor her children ever saw John Walker Parkman again. But he remained in the memory of my grandmother, Johnnie Mae, who recalled taking him glasses of ice water at her mother's direction as he worked in the fields. Those faint memories were her only inheritance from her father, who she saw for the last time when she was five years old.

John Parkman died at 76 years of age, and Jessie died, hundreds of miles away and 30 years later just shy of her 80th birthday. Despite decades of opportunity to do so, neither of them ever married other spouses. When she moved North, she assumed his name as hers, reporting to the 1930 census taker that she was Jessie Lee Parkman. He died with her name on his lips; and she died with his name and his image, the one and only item of hers that now belongs to me.

It was during the summer of my freshman year at Valparaiso University that I went to Chicago with my mother to visit Aunt Mary, my Grandma Jessie's little sister. She was the second and last of the two children of Kitty and Dennis Mahone. It was 1984. She was 80 years old at the time and still living in the South-Side apartment that she'd first rented when she arrived in Chicago nearly 60 years before. It was during that visit that Aunt Mary shared her eyewitness account of the unlikely, mysterious, and ill-fated bond without which I would not exist.

In 2007, I took the youngest surviving child of John and Jessie Parkman to meet his White family members. At 83 years old, my Uncle Willie Parkman travelled with me to Opelika, Alabama, to connect with a part of his identity that he had never known. There, we met his first cousin, Mary Parkman Colman, John Parkman's 85-year-old niece. It struck me that Cousin Mary, as I came to call her, was virtually the identical twin of my grandmother, Johnnie Mae. She was spritely and talkative, and shared story after story of my great-grandfather, for whom she cared during the last years of his life. I told her about her Uncle John's "Jess," and she shared pictures and letters with me and her Black cousin, my Uncle Willie, for several years following until she died.

During that trip, Uncle Willie and I drove over to nearby Pittsview to see the land where his mother and her family might have worked as sharecroppers. We saw remnants of Prudence Crossing, including a street sign marking the location of Prudence Road. Nearby were acres and acres of farmland, the remains of a general store, and an old, abandoned depot. I imagined the depot in its heyday and wondered whether it might have been the last place Grandma Jessie stood before boarding the "Colored" section of the passenger train to bring her young children North.

We then crossed the state line to Georgia to visit the grave of John Walker Parkman. I stood a short distance away, respecting the gravity of that sacred moment between my aged uncle and his father. We were in no hurry; I gave them space and time. After all, it had been 81 years.

Perhaps Dr. Martin Luther King, Jr. said it best in his *Letter from a Birmingham Jail*: "We are caught in an inescapable network of mutuality, tied in a single garment of destiny." Like it or not, we are family. How we came to be family does not erase the fact that we are. The original owners of this land were those Native American people from whom land was systematically stolen. Now, we are all here, and this land, to all of us, is home. And home is far from perfect. Our American home has been the scene of suffering, abuse, and oppression. Yet, it is a place of possibility—possibility that resides in the beauty of our diversity and our willingness to reach beyond the boundaries of our fears and our ignorance. We are dysfunctional, and as a nation, we have been largely oblivious to many of the deeper truths of our national identity; still, we are a great country. There is a rich and untapped reservoir of meaning and connectedness for White people who dare to acknowledge the utter impossibility of the American story without African American people and other people of color. And there can be greater movement toward healing, wholeness, and trust for African American people who dare to see the possibility for change in the kind of courageous White people who've read this book. Racism is fueled by fear, and fear is fueled by ignorance. And ignorance melts—one curious mind and one honest answer at a time.

John Walker Parkman. In 2007 (57 years after his death), the Alabama Parkman family first came to know of his 25 African American descendants.
(This photo is circa 1910. Author's collection.)

Jessie Lee Mahone Parkman. She sat for this photograph soon after migrating from Prudence Crossing, Alabama, to Chicago, Illinois, in the late 1920s.

(This photo is circa 1926. Author's collection.)

Jessie Lee Mahone Parkman (seated first row, third from right, wearing corsage), celebrating her 64th birthday with her family in Gary, Indiana. To her right are her daughter, Johnnie Mae Parkman, and her son, Willie Parkman. To her immediate left is her younger sister, Mary, and second from her left is her youngest daughter, Katherine Parkman Hunter. Seated farthest to the left is Tobi Lorraine Upshaw Shelton (pregnant with the author.) Standing in second row, farthest left, is the author's father, Lee Shelton, who is holding the author's oldest sister, Terralyn Shelton (Roach).

(This photo is dated 1964. Source: Author's collection.)

Willie Parkman, age 96, holding a fifth-generation descendant of his parents, John Walker Parkman and Jessie Lee Mahone Parkman.

(This photo was taken in 2020. Author's collection.)

Appendix

On June 3, 2020, I sent the following letter to the faculty, staff, and students in the University of Louisville School of Music as a response to racial unrest in our city and around the country.

Friends;

I will soon celebrate my first year at the University of Louisville. Traveling cross-country to begin anew was no small feat. After twenty-five rewarding years at The University of Tulsa, the move entailed many uncertainties, and a risk that I now know was well worth taking. I am a proud Cardinal, and my connections here with students, faculty, staff, and administrative colleagues are richer and more precious to me than I ever could have imagined. I am deeply grateful.

Within months of joining the Cardinal Family, I find myself bonded to this community in ways that are perhaps intensified by this time of global unease. In early March, the pronounced threat of COVID-19 caused us to quickly convert to online teaching. Our faculty were nimble and resourceful in managing this abrupt change, and our students were real troopers, sheltering in place as they received music instruction online, some completing their degrees in May. As we continue to face the threat of this global health crisis, we now face another crisis, one that is not new, but that has reached a dangerous boiling point given the convergence of recent tragic events.

The headlines on racial unrest require that influential voices bring messages of unity and hope. On May 29th, President

Bendapudi did just that. In her email to our campus community, she affirmed our institutional identity as a Community of Care and our embrace of diversity, equity, and inclusion. In follow up to her affirmation, I offer these reflections to my School of Music Family with the intent of ensuring the prevalence of authenticity, safety, compassion, and friendship within our walls.

As a person of color in a role of leadership and visibility, I am in a state of constant internal negotiation, balancing my professional persona with this other reality of my existence that is well beyond the sanctuary of academia. For example, I speak of COVID-19 using statistics with deliberate calm and a measured, objective tone. Meanwhile, the virus hits close to home. A close friend of mine and the long-time music minister at my church contacted me in March as he sped to be at his father's bedside. One of the first that I knew personally to succumb to the virus, his dad lived in Flint, Michigan, where disadvantaged communities of color there have long sought access to clean water.

Even as I write this, I find myself negotiating, sifting through a pile of words, collecting some, tossing others aside, trying to decide just what to express about the state of racial injustice at this volatile moment in our country's history. Whatever words land in this message, I hope for two outcomes: First, I hope that my candor and transparency point a way forward for all of us, helping to facilitate the healing that our community wants and so desperately needs. Secondly, I hope that the spirit of my discourse affirms the basic goodness of humanity in which I so firmly believe.

One of the thousands of photos on my iPhone was uploaded in September of 2016. To understand the significance of the photo, I must take you back to the joyous and spirited rehearsals I attended every Saturday at noon with the Unlimited Praise Gospel Choir on the campus of the University of Tulsa in the early 1990s. The musician for the gospel choir was a very soft-spoken musical genius named Joey Crutcher. Joey was one of the local ambassadors of the Gospel Music Workshops of America, an international organization that supports and disseminates black gospel music all over the world. From the piano, Joey taught our choir a wealth of repertoire week after week, and he traveled with us to do numerous singing engagements at churches and community events around the city and region. The Crutcher family was well known and highly regarded, and Joey was a treasured friend to many of us. He was the musician at my wedding in 1996.

The photo on my iPhone is from a police dashcam. It is time-stamped September 16, 2016, at 7:43 pm. Pictured is a black man wearing a white t-shirt with both of his arms raised in surrender; he is standing to the left of a stalled vehicle in the middle of the road, and he is faced forward, away from the camera, his back to the officers who are a few feet behind him. Within moments after that photograph was taken, Officer Betty Shelby discharged her weapon, shooting and killing the black man whose hands were in the air. He had no weapon. That man was Terence Crutcher. He was Joey Crutcher's son.

Despite the evidence captured on camera—that Terence had no weapon, posed no threat, and was only stopped in the street because his car stalled—ultimately, no one was ever held accountable for his death. There was outrage. There were protests in the streets of Tulsa, calling for Shelby's arrest. There was a trial. Betty Shelby was not only acquitted, but her record was expunged of the incident. She was hired by a neighboring Oklahoma county, where she has since been teaching law enforcement classes. The local news did a story on heroic officers, and Betty Shelby was the featured guest.

The worldwide protests dominating our headlines today are not just for George Floyd, Breonna Taylor, or Ahmaud Arbery; they are protests against a system of brutality and inequality that extends back generations. This system normalizes, particularly for black men, a macabre cause-and-effect relationship between routine acts of everyday living (like stopping at a 7-Eleven for a bag of Skittles, or going for a jog, or seeking help with a flat tire) and the probability of a violent death at the hands of law enforcement. Each glance at that photo of Terence's last moments of life brings me another micro dose of grief.

Terence's death, George's death, Breonna's death, and Ahmaud's death are all part of a pattern that now seems to garner a predictable reaction, followed by a national shrug of the shoulders before things revert to the status quo. Countless unarmed people of color have met with a similar demise at the hands of officers, and some of the higher-profile victims within the past six or seven years have included Trayvon Martin, Eric Garner, Dontre Hamilton, John Crawford, III, Michael Brown, Ezell Ford, Tanisha Anderson, Tamir Rice, Tony Robinson, Phillip White, Eric Harris, Walter Scott, and Freddie Gray. In the 1950s and 1960s, television was the new technology that enabled eyewitnesses to record and disseminate evidence of the treatment of blacks in the Jim Crow South. Today, the technology that captures the racially charged brutality that would otherwise go unnoticed is the Smartphone. The evidence explains why African Americans live with the daily realization that the mere perception that we pose a threat could cost us our lives.

On July 6, 2016, Philando Castile was pulled over by a police officer and was shot and killed as he reached for his license and registration. I know that law enforcement can kill my husband, my father, my uncles, my nephews, my brothers-in-law, my students of color, and me without a good reason, and that they can do so without consequence. As Amy Cooper recently demonstrated during the now-infamous incident in Central Park, there is a clear and common understanding of how incredibly vulnerable people of color are at the hands of the police. Guilty or not, threat or not, history has proven that any encounter we have with the police potentially places our lives in the balance.

For a very long time, this uncomfortable reality was never one that emerged with any degree of authenticity in my conversations with my white colleagues and friends. That all changed the day after Officer Betty Shelby's acquittal for Terence Crutcher's murder. When the verdict was announced, the entire city of Tulsa seemed as racially polarized as it had been during its infamous 1921 Race Massacre. I was shocked and appalled when colleagues with whom I'd worked for many years seemed satisfied, even relieved with the verdict, believing that Terence—whose character by then had been spun into an entirely fabricated, incriminating narrative—had gotten what he deserved. I had to expend enormous amounts of mental, emotional, and psychological energy just to keep from becoming consumed with despair and hatred. That's when I decided to take a risk.

I have a friend who is white and remains to this day one of my dearest buddies and closest colleagues in Music. She and I had worked and taught together for over twenty years. I taught her son and watched her kids grow up. We joined each other for decadent meals at breakfast or lunch on a fairly regular basis. Over the years, we'd have our fitness binges, meeting at the track to walk, or at the Y for yoga, all excuses to talk and just enjoy spending time together. We kept each other laughing, finished each other's sentences, and whenever we had the chance to hang out, the time seemed to pass too quickly. We talked about everything. Everything, that is, except race.

We in the black community are very well practiced at grieving together and consoling each other. This time, however, I needed to locate, affirm, and draw upon humanity in my white colleagues and friends. During the time of this tragedy, I needed to know that they were really friends, and not just superficial acquaintances for whom I was the checked-off box on a diversity list. Afraid, angry, and unsure, I took out my cell phone that day and I sent her a simple, four-word text: "I am not well."

Right now, black people in this country "are not well". Our titles, our positions, our achievements notwithstanding, we as a community "are not well". We have spent our entire lives learning the history and mastering the norms, customs, and standards that emanate from a Euro-American lens. We survive and succeed only because we adapt. Conversely, even some of the most well-intentioned and good-hearted white friends and colleagues among us have, at best, a fraction of a clue as to why race is fraught with such tension and pain. They mentally ascent to diversity policies, and they dutifully recite all of the politically correct diversity and inclusion mantras; yet they've spent precious little time learning the history and understanding the norms, customs, and survival mechanisms that inform the way many black people view and experience the world. With only surface knowledge of our history, and with little incentive to dig deeper, we remain stuck in a cycle. Another weaponless black man is killed, there is an outcry, there are protests, but nothing really changes. Things quiet down, and then the cycle repeats. Another weaponless black man is killed, there is an outcry, there are protests . . . .

But here's what gives me stubborn hope. I sent my friend the text, and I held my breath, unsure as to how she'd respond, as we'd never been down that path before in our friendship. And then, the dam broke. Literally within seconds, she responded, understanding full well from just those four words exactly what I meant. She urgently flooded me with the love of a sister who feared neither my brokenness nor my blackness. And our conversations changed. She admitted that she knew me, but didn't really know me, my people, my culture, my history; and that she wanted to correct that. Soon, her vulnerability matched mine, and she started asking honest questions, and I answered her without judgment or ridicule because her sincerity empowered me to do so. Her ignorance about my history was not her fault, but she made seeking this knowledge her responsibility. She started to read, to learn, and to impact others, and she did so, not as a perfunctory Band-Aid, but as a matter of heartfelt commitment to making the world better. She became a safe place for me, and I for her. We began to heal each other, and to this day, her friendship continues to be a highly valued source of support for me.

Policies may govern behavior. Policies alone, however, don't change hearts. Through the anger that I feel whenever human life is devalued, I persist in my conviction that most of the people are good. I believe that the overwhelming majority of white people are kind and concerned, but many may be profoundly confused. They know that racism is bad, and yet they are flooded with images and stories that depict black people as dangerous and destructive societal burdens who are ultimately disposable. Many have only a shallow awareness of the African American story, an awareness so frail that it can hardly compete with the powerful onslaught of misinformation that normalizes the unwarranted destruction of our lives.

The only remedy for ignorance is education. And so, for my white colleagues, students, associates, and others who wish to move beyond that awkward, uncomfortable space where the genuine desire to do good sits in stagnant conflict with uncertainty about where to start, I offer practical help. To white people, I say notice your circle and see the people of color in your life whose healing depends upon your willingness to be vulnerable. To black people, I say look beyond the madness and locate, among your circle of white colleagues, peers, and friends, the spaces where you can take a calculated risk to be open and honest about your pain with those who may genuinely care. To those who would admit to the gaps in your knowledge of the African American story, I say fix it—not in one rally, or one protest, but fix it with commitment over time. The UofL Office of Diversity and Equity offers programs, training, and resources in diversity, equity and inclusion, and social justice. Those who wish might also begin this learning journey by viewing ROOTS, the miniseries based on the memoir by Alex Haley. (There are two different versions of the miniseries, but either will do.) From there, consider viewing Twelve Years a Slave, The Help, The Butler, 42, and Selma. For reading, begin with The Souls of Black Folk by W.E.B. DuBois, and The New Jim Crow by Michelle Alexander. Additional readings are I'm Still Here: Black Dignity in a World Made for Whiteness, by Austin Channing Brown; How to be an Antiracist by Ibram X Kendi; So You Want to Talk About Race, by Ijeomo Oluo, and Me and White Supremacy: Combat Racism, Change the World, and Become a Good Ancestor by Layla Saad. Learning takes time and commitment, but this is nothing to despair. Black people start learning about whiteness at birth. The more we all learn about each other, the more effectively we can break the patterns that sicken our society.

I envision that, in our best world, our racial climate results not from policies and mandates handed down from administrative thrones, but from heart-changes fueled by vulnerability, honesty, authenticity, and true friendship. For any who would seek to know the deeper reasons behind the trouble that fills our news, I offer myself as a safe space, an accepting heart and a nonjudgmental listening ear for all people who want to transcend broken patterns. If there is interest, I am also more than willing to schedule a series of "safe place" discussions and informal listening sessions so that good people who wish to move us all toward a better reality can collaborate in achieving that objective. I envision that we have the power to grow into a community where any one of us can send a four-word text message and we will all have the skills necessary to respond with trust and love regardless of race, religion, sexual *orientation, gender identity, national origin, or any other identifier. We often refer to the SOM as a family. It is important that we live the essential meaning of "family" by becoming a true component of support during these times as we navigate and heal together.*

I thumb through the photos on my iPhone and get a glimpse of Terence Crutcher. I also get glimpses of hundreds of family photos that prove the transcendence of authenticity, honesty, and friendship. I see my two white nieces, my two Puerto-Rican nephews, and their beautiful children, and I think through my tears that this is possible.

Warmly,
Teresa

Acknowledgments

Many perspectives were critical to the completion of this manuscript. I am deeply grateful to Dr. Susan E. Chase, Vernon Howard, Kimberly Johnson, Dr. Crystal L. Keels, David Miller, Terralyn Roach, Brooklyn Russell, and Melanie Maina for their careful reading of the developing draft of this book and for their useful feedback, insights, and suggestions.

I am indebted to Karen and Jerry for their feedback and support when I penned my first thoughts on race to the University of Louisville Cardinal Family.

I extend my sincerest thanks to Dr. Neeli Bendapudi for making it safe for me to write and share this book. I am inspired by her bold leadership and decisive embrace of an antiracist agenda for the University of Louisville.

I am grateful for the Black people and the White people in my life who have transcended their own comfort zones to find higher levels of harmony and community. My deepest thanks to the "Safe Saturday" crew for their courageous conversations about race.

My eternal thanks to Dana for speaking powerful words at a critical moment (and for equally well-timed Irish soda bread).

Finally, I am forever indebted to James, who is my pillow, my rock, and my partner for life.

NOTES

Introduction

1. Stanglin, Doug. "Auction Ends for Gun That Killed Trayvon Martin." *USA Today*, 18 May 2016, https://www.usatoday.com/story/news/2016/05/18/auction-ends-gun-killed-trayvon-martin/84547144/.

2. Jones, Corey. "Betty Shelby Teaching Course for Officers on 'Surviving the Aftermath of a Critical Incident'." *Tulsa World*, 24 Aug. 2018.

3. Other scholars have published treatments of race, racism, and racial difference with much more sophistication, rigor, and nuance than I intend to present in this book. See, for example, Kendi, Ibram X. *How to Be an Antiracist*. Random House, 2020.

Chapter 2

1. Morava, Maria and Scottie Andrew. "An Indiana University Retires Its Mascot That Shares a Name with the Ku Klux Klan Newspaper." *CNN*, 12 Feb. 2021, https://www.cnn.com/2021/02/12/us/ valparaiso-university-mascot-trnd/index.html.

Chapter 3

1. Numerous news outlets featured this quote from Trump. See, for example, Jackson, David "Trump Says He's the 'Least Racist Person' in the World, Sees Joe Biden as Democratic Debate Favorite." *USA Today*, 30 July 2019. Also Dorman, John L. "Trump Claims He is 'the Least Racist Person in This Room' to Biden and a Black Moderator at the Final Presidential Debate." *Business Insider*, 22 Oct. 2020, https://www.businessinsider.com/donald-trump-joe-biden-racism-race-relations-presidential-debate-video-2020-10.

2. Tani, Maxwell. "Wolf Blitzer Grills Donald Trump: Why are White Supremacists Supporting You?" *Business Insider*, 21 Mar. 2016, https: //www.businessinsider.com / wolf - blitzer- donald – trump - donald-trump-cnn-interview-2016-3.

Chapter 6

1. Woodlee, Yolanda. "Williams Aide Resigns in Language Dispute." *The Washington Post*, 27 Jan. 1999, https://www.washingtonpost. com/wp-srv/local/daily/jan99/district27.htm.

2. Definition of *niggardly* from *Dictionary.com*. Accessed 30 Mar. 2021, https://www.dictionary.com/browse/niggardly?s=t.

3. Woodlee, "Williams Aide Resigns in Language Dispute."

4. See dramatization of the Tuskegee Experiment in the 1997 film, *Ms. Evers' Boys*, directed by Joseph Sargent.

5. See the stories of Elaine Riddick of North Carolina, Minnie Lee and Mary Alice Relf of Alabama, et al. Zucchino, David. "Sterilized by North Carolina, She Felt Raped Once More." *Los Angeles Times*, 25 Jan. 2012, https://www.latimes.com/archives/la-xpm-2012-jan-25-la-na-forced-sterilization-20120126-story.html. See also Threadcraft, Shatema. *Intimate Justice: the Black Female Body and the Body Politic.* Oxford University Press, 2018.

6. For a more comprehensive discussion of African American history, I highly recommend the six-part documentary *The African Americans* (2013) and its companion book by the same name (2016). The series covers over five centuries, and its installments include "The Black Atlantic (1500–1800);" "The Age of Slavery (1800–1860);" "Into the Fire (1861–1896);" "Making a Way out of No Way (1897–1940);" "Rise! (1940–1968)," and "A More Perfect Union (1968–2013)." See Gates, Henry Louis, et al., directors. *The African Americans: Many Rivers to Cross.* PBS, 2013. See also the first-person narrative of Solomon Northup, *Twelve Years a Slave* (originally published in 1853) and the 2013 film by the same name featuring Chiwetel Ejiofor as Northup, Steve McQueen, director. Alex Haley's *Roots: The Saga of an American Family*, originally published in 1976 (Doubleday), depicts one Black family's story from its African ancestral roots to modern times and is widely considered to be a representative telling of Black history. *Roots* has twice been presented in mini-series format, first in 1977, and later in 2007 (see Marvin J. Chomsky, et.al, directors, *Roots.*

Warner Bros. Television, 1977, and Margulies, Stan, et al. *Roots.* Warner Home Video, 2007).

7. The murders of George Floyd, Breonna Taylor, Ahmaud Arbery, and many others were widely covered by national news outlets. Information is readily available online.

8. Alexander, Michelle. *The New Jim Crow: Mass Incarceration in the Age of Colorblindness.* New Press, 2020.

9. Starr, Sonja B. and M.M. Rehavi."Racial Disparity in Federal Criminal Sentences." *Journal of Political Economy*, 122, no. 6 (2014): 1320-54.

Chapter 7

1. Remnick, Noah. "Yale Grapples with Ties to Slavery in Debate Over a College's Name." *The New York Times*, 11 Sept. 2015.

2. Ojalvo, Holly Epstein. "Beyond Yale: These Other University Buildings Have Ties to Slavery and White Supremacy." *USA TODAY*, 13 Feb. 2017.

3. McIntosh, Kriston, Emily Moss, Ryan Nunn, and Jay Shambaugh. "Examining the Black White Wealth Gap." *Brookings Institute,* 27 Feb. 2020.

Chapter 8

1. See Lineberry, Cate. *Be Free or Die: The Amazing Story of Robert Smalls' Escape from Slavery to Union Hero.* Picador, 2018.

2. Gates, Henry Louis and Evelyn Brooks Higginbotham. *The African American National Biography.* Oxford University Press, 2008. (Subsequent hardcover editions were published in 2012 and 2013, respectively. It is also offered online as part of the Oxford African American Study Center.)

3. See the table "Percentage of Persons 14 Years Old and Over Who Were Illiterate (Unable to Read or Write in Any Language), by Race

and Nativity: 1870 to 1979" from *U.S. Department of Commerce, Bureau of the Census, Historical Statistics of the United States, Colonial Times to 1970; and Current Population Reports, Series P-23, Ancestry and Language in the United States: November 1979.* This table, which was prepared in September 1992, shows that for decades following the end of slavery, African Americans remained more than twice as likely to be illiterate than White people, Native American people, and immigrants.

4. Douglass, Margaret Crittenden. *Educational Laws of Virginia; The Personal Narrative of Mrs. Margaret Douglass, a Southern Woman, who was Imprisoned for One Month in the Common Jail of Norfolk, Under the Laws of Virginia, for the Crime of Teaching Free Colored Children to Read.* Jewett and Worthington, 1854.

5. McGoldrick, Thomas Joseph, Sister. *Beyond the Call: The Legacy of the Sisters of St. Joseph of St. Augustine, Florida.* Xlibris Corporation, 2007.

6. Nichols, John. "Why the Hell Is the Supreme Court Allowing a New Poll Tax to Disenfranchise Florida Voters?" *The Nation,* 17 July 2020, https://www.thenation.com/article/politics/supreme-court-florida-felony-voting-rights/.

7. American Civil Liberties Union. "Block the Vote: Voter Suppression in 2020." 3 Feb. 2020, https://www.aclu.org/news/civil-liberties/block-the-vote-voter-suppression-in-2020/.

8. Multiple major news outlets reported on the new restrictions included in Georgia's March 2021 voting law. Details of the law are readily available online.

9. See Brown, DeNeen L. "All-Black Towns Across America: Life Was Hard but Full of Promise." *The Washington Post,* 27 Mar. 2015, https://www.washingtonpost.com/lifestyle/style/a-list-of-well-known-black-towns/2015/03/27/9f21ca42-cdc4-11e4-a2a7-9517a3a70506_story.html.

10. Feldman, Amy and Luisa Kroll. "100 Black-Owned Businesses to Support" *Forbes,* 5 June 2020, https://www.forbes.com/sites/

elisabethbrier/2020/06/05/100-black-owned-businesses-to-support
/?sh=1147f103660d.

Chapter 9

1. See Tucker, John. "10 of the Most Affluent African American Suburbs in the Nation." *Black Enterprise*, 21 Nov. 2017, https:// www.blackenterprise.com/10-affluent-african-american-suburbs/.

2. See Rothstein, Richard. *The Color of Law: A Forgotten History of How our Government Segregated America.* Liveright Publishing Corporation, a Division of W.W. Norton & Company, 2018.

3. Ibid.

4. Wise, Robert and Jerome Robbins. *West Side Story*, 1961.

5. Miller, Walter B. "Violent Crimes in City Gangs." *The Annals of the American Academy of Political and Social Science*, vol. 364, Mar. 1966, pp. 97–113.

6. Hardman, Dale G. "Small Town Gangs." *The Journal of Criminal Law, Criminology, and Police Science*, vol. 60, no. 2, 1969, p. 173.

Chapter 10

1. Bronson, Po and Ashley Merryman. "Even Babies Discriminate: A Nurtureshock Excerpt." *Newsweek Magazine*, 4 Sept. 2009.

2. Frey, William H. *Diversity Explosion: How New Racial Demographics are Remaking America.* Brookings Institution Press, 2018.

3. Frey, William H. "Less Than Half of US Children Under 15 are White, Census Shows."*Brookings Institute* (report), 24 June 2019, https:// www.brookings.edu/research/less-than-half-of-us-children-under-15-are-White-census-shows/.

4. Curtis, Mary C. "Strom Thurmond's Black Daughter: A Symbol of America's Complicated Racial History." *The Washington Post*, 5 Feb. 2013,https://www.washingtonpost.com/blogs /she-the-people/wp/

2013/ 02/ 05 / strom-thurmonds-black-daughter-a-flesh-and-blood-symbol-of-americas - complicated -racial – history/.

See also Washington-Williams, Essie Mae, and William Stadiem. *Dear Senator: A Memoir by the Daughter of Strom Thurmond.* HarperCollins, 2005.

5. Geiger, A.W., and Gretchen Livingston. "8 Facts about Love and Marriage in America." Pew Research Center, 21 Aug. 2020, www. pewresearch. org / fact-tank / 2019/ 02/13/8 -facts-about-love-and-marriage/.

Chapter 11

1. See Blackmon, Douglas A. *Slavery by Another Name: The Re-Enslavement of Black Americans from the Civil War to World War II.* Doubleday, 2008. See also Alexander, Michelle. *The New Jim Crow: Mass Incarceration in the Age of Colorblindness.* New Press, 2020.

2. Assefa, Lydette, S. "Assessing Dangerousness Amidst Racial Stereotypes: An Analysis of the Role of Racial Bias in Bond Decisions and Ideas for Reform." *Journal of Criminal Law & Criminology*, vol. 108, no. 4, 2018.

3. See Waxman, Olivia B. "President Trump Played a Key Role in the Central Park Five Case: Here's the Real History Behind *When They See Us.*" *Time Magazine,* 31 May 2019, https://time.com/5597843/central-park-five-trump-history/.

4. The stories of Susan Smith, the Philadelphia Starbucks incident, Jermaine Massey, and Amy Cooper were all widely covered on national news outlets. Information regarding these occurrences is readily available online.

5. Ibid.

6. Ibid.

7. Ibid.

8. Elfrink, Tim. "A Teacher Saw a BB Gun in a 9-Year-Old's Room During Online Class. He Faced Expulsion."*The Washington Post*, 25 Sept. 2020, https://www.washingtonpost.com/nation/2020/09/25/louisiana-student-bbgun-expulsion/.

9. Neal, La Vonne I., et al. "The Effects of African American Movement Styles on Teachers' Perceptions and Reactions." *Journal of Special Education*, vol. 37, no. 1, Spring 2003, pp. 49–57.

10. Gilliam, Walter S., et al. "Do Early Educators' Implicit Biases Regarding Sex and Race Relate to Behavior Expectations and Recommendations of Preschool Expulsions and Suspensions?" Yale Child Study Center, 2016.

11. Merelli, Annalisa. "The Darker Your Skin, the More Likely You'll End up in an American Jail." This Harvard study was reported in *Quartz* on Yahoo Finance, 16 Oct. 2019, https://finance.yahoo.com/news/darker-skin-more-likely-ll-110017965.html).

12. Rehavi, M. Marit, and Sonja B. Starr. "Racial Disparity in Federal Criminal Sentences." *Journal of Political Economy*, vol. 122, no. 6, Dec. 2014, pp. 1320–1354. See also *The New Jim Crow* and *Slavery by Another Name*, cited previously.

Chapter 12

1. Dr. Laura's use of the "N" word was widely reported in national news sources. Both this coverage and the actual audio of the incident are readily available online.

2. Pope Nicholas V. *Dum Diversas*. Papal bull issued 18 June 1452.

3. Roediger, David R. "Historical Foundations of Race." *National Museum of African American History and Culture*, 20 July 2020, nmaahc.si.edu/learn/ talking-about-race/topics/ historical-foundations-race.

4. Mather, Cotton. "The Negro Christianized." Bartholomew Green, 1706.

5. See Kennedy, Randall. *Nigger: The Strange Career of a Troublesome Word.* Knopf Doubleday Publishing Group, 2008.

Chapter 13

1. Bigg, Matthew. "Election of Obama Provokes Rise in U.S. Hate Crimes." *Reuters*, 24 Nov. 2008.

2. "Obama Win Sparks Rise in Hate Crimes, Violence." *National Public Radio*, 25 Nov. 2008, https://www.npr.org/templates/story/story.php?storyId=97454237.

3. The "Birtherism" conspiracy received wide coverage both before and during Barack Obama's presidency. Examples of this coverage include the following:

   Rutenberg, Jim. "The Man Behind the Whispers About Obama." *The New York Times*, 12 Oct. 2008, https://www.nytimes.com/2008/10/13/us/politics/13martin.html; "Will 'Birther' Issue Now Be Put to Rest?" *USA Today*, 29 Apr. 2011; Johnson, Jenna. "Trump Admits Obama Was Born in U.S., But Falsely Blames Clinton for Starting Rumors." *The Washington Post*, 16 Sept. 2016, https://www.washingtonpost.com/news/post- politics /wp/2016/09/16/ trump- admits- obama- was- born- in- u- s- but- falsely- blames- clinton- for- starting-rumors/.

4. Tumulty, Karen, Kate Woodsome, and Sergio Pecanha. "How Sexist, Racist Attacks on Kamala Harris Have Spread Online— A Case Study." *The Washington Post*, 7 Oct. 2020.

5. Ulloa, Jazmine. "As Kamala Harris Faces Racist and Sexist Online Attacks, Women's Groups and Democratic Operatives Say They Have Her Back." The Boston Globe, 12 Aug. 2020, www.bostonglobe.com /2020/08/12/nation/ kamala- harris- faces- racist- sexist-online-attacks-womens-groups-democratic-operatives-say-they -have-her-back/.

Chapter 14

1. DenHoed, Andrea. "The Forgotten Lessons of the American Eugenics Movement." *The New Yorker*, 27 Apr. 2016.

2. McCord, Charles H. *The American Negro as a Dependent, Defective, and Delinquent.* Benson Printing Company, 1914, p. 40.

3. Tracy, Jan. "News Media Offers Consistently Warped Portrayals of Black Families, Study Finds." *The Washington Post*, 13 Dec. 2017, https://www.washingtonpost.com /news/wonk/wp/2017/12/13/ news-media-offers-consistently-warped-portrayals-of-Black-families-study-finds/.

4. Keyes, Allison. "The East St. Louis Race Riot Left Dozens Dead, Devastating a Community on the Rise." *Smithsonian Magazine*, 30 June 2017, https:// www.smithsonianmag.com/smithsonian-institution/ east-st-louis-race-riot- left- dozens-dead-devastating- community-on-the-rise-180963885/.

5. Moyer, Justin Wm. "White Student Made 'Co-Valedictorian' With Black Student, Despite Having Lower GPA, Lawsuit Claims." *The Washington Post*, 20 June 2017, https://www.washingtonpost.com/ news /education /wp/ 2017/06/30/white-student-made-co-valedictorian-with-black-student-despite-having-lower-gpa-lawsuit-claims/.

Chapter 15

1. Cole, Nicki Lisa. "9 Surprising Facts About Welfare Recipients." ThoughtCo, 11 June 2020, www.thoughtco.com / who-really-receives-welfare-4126592.

2. Demby, Gene. "The Truth Behind the Lies of the Original 'Welfare Queen.'" Code Switch, National Public Radio. Heard on *All Things Considered*, 20 Dec. 2013, https://www.npr.org/sections/codeswitch /2013/12/20/255819681/ the-truth-behind-the-lies-of-the-original-welfare-queen.

3. Ibid.

4. Pager, Devah. "The Mark of a Criminal Record." *American Journal of Sociology*, vol. 108, no. 5, 2003.

Chapter 16

1. The Fisher case was widely covered. See Liptak, Adam. "Supreme Court Upholds Affirmative Action Program at University of Texas." *The New York Times*, 23 June 2016.

Chapter 18

1. O'Neill, Aaron. "Number of Slaves Owned by U.S. Presidents 1789-1877." Statista.com, 29 July 2020, https: // www. statista.com / statistics/1121963/slaves-owned-by-us-presidents/.

2. Hill, Bob. "A Long History of Faith and Survival." *Courier Journal*, 4 Oct. 2014, https: // www. courier-journal.com/ story/ opinion/ contributors/2014/10/04/long-history-faith-survival/16662017/.

3. Baptist, Edward E. *The Half Has Never Been Told: Slavery and the Making of American Capitalism.* Basic Books, 2014, pp. 11–16.

4. "15 Major Corporations You Never Knew Profited from Slavery." *Atlanta Black Star*, 26 Aug. 2013, https:// atlantaBlackpeopletar. com/ 2013/08/ 26/ 17 -major- companies- never- knew- benefited- slavery/6/.

5. Ibid.

6. See Williams, Shannen Dee. "The Church Must Make Reparation for Its Role in Slavery, Segregation." *National Catholic Reporter*, 15 June 2020, https://www.ncronline.org/news/opinion/church-must-make -reparation-its-role-slavery-segregation.

7. See Hassan, Adeel. "Oldest Institution of Southern Baptist Convention Reveals Past Ties to Slavery." *The New York Times*, 12 Dec. 2018, https: //www.nytimes.com /2018/12/12/us/southern- baptist-slavery.html.

8. Wilkins, Erica, et al. "Residual Effects of Slavery: What Clinicians Need to Know." *Contemporary Family Therapy: An International Journal*, vol. 35, no. 1, 2013, https://doi.org/10.1007/s10591-012-9219-1.

9. Ibid., 17–18.

10. Ibid., 18.

Chapter 19

1. The Oklahoma City Bombing, the early mention of Middle Eastern terrorism, and the subsequent arrest of Timothy McVeigh were all widely reported on multiple national news outlets. That information is readily accessible online.

2. The killing of Philando Castile was widely reported on multiple national news outlets. This story is readily available online.

3. Many online sources maintain lists of unarmed people of color killed in officer and/or vigilante-involved and situations. A few of these sources are as follows:

   https://www.reneeater.com/on-monuments-blog/tag/list+of+unarmed+Black+people+killed+by+police

   https:// www.cbsnews.com/ news/ say- their- names- list- people-injured-killed-police-officer-involved-incidents/

   https://www.bbc.com/news/world-us-canada-52905408

   https: //www.npr.org /2020/ 05/ 29/ 865261916/ a- decade- of-watching-Black-people-die

Chapter 20

1. Atwater, Ann. "What Forgiveness Costs." Initially published in the *Durham Herald Sun*, 15 Dec. 2013, https://www.schoolforconversion. org/ann-atwaterin-her-own-words.

2. Smith, Ben. "Sen. Robert Byrd Endorses Obama." Politico, 19 May 2008, https: // www.politico.com/ blogs/ben-smith/2008/05/sen-robert-byrd-endorses-obama-008895.

3. Michaelis, Arno. *My Life After Hate*. Authentic Presence Publications, 2012.

Chapter 21

1. Thornton, William. "More than 300 African-Americans Lynched in Alabama in 66 Years." *Al.com*, 6 Mar. 2019, https://www.al.com/news/2018/04/alabamas_racial_lynching_victi.html.

2. *Ku Klux Klan: A History of Racism and Violence*. The Klanwatch Project of the Southern Poverty Law Center, 2011.

3. Thornton, William. "More than 300 African-Americans Lynched in Alabama in 66 Years."

4. Ibid.

INDEX

(Note: Page numbers in *italics* refer to illustrations.)

Aetna Insurance, 132
affirmative action, 119–23
  consideration of race in college
    admissions, 120–21
  as corrective, 121, 123
  unintended consequences of, 122–23
  White opposition to, 120, 122, 168
African American National Biography, 52
African Americans (term), 28
African people, perceived as inferior, 91–92
Alabama
  lynchings in, 172–73, 177
  Prudence Crossing community, 170–71, 174, 182–83
Alcis, Carlos, 146
Alexander, Michelle, 41–42
Allen, Clinton R., 146
Allen, Raymond Luther, Jr., 148
Allen, Wendell James, 147
All Souls Unitarian Church in Tulsa, Oklahoma, 155
American Civil Liberties Union (ACLU), 57
American Journal of Sociology, 117
The American Negro as a Dependent, Defective, and Delinquent (McCord), 107–8
amnesia, Black elders' practice of intentional, 169–70
ancestry of African Americans, 131
Anderson, Tanisha N., 144, 193
anger of Black people, 33–42

about exploitation of Black bodies, 40–41
about inequality, 36–39
and mass incarceration of Black people, 36, 41–42
and "niggardly" term employed by Howard, 33–34
and protests publicized in media, 34
and systemic racism, 39–40
antisemitism, 19–20
Arbery, Ahmaud
  death of, xii, xiv, 193
  and protests, 34, 192
arrests in Black communities, 36, 41–42
Ashley, Alonzo, Jr., 148
Asian people, 70
Assefa, Lydette, 76
Atwater, Ann, 155–56
Aurora, Colorado, theatre shooting (2012), 64

Bailey, Aaron, 142
Baker, Jordan, 145
Bendapudi, Neeli, xiii, 190
The Best of Enemies (film), 156
Biden, Joseph, 19, 99
Bigler, Rebecca, 68–69
birth/death certificates of Black people, 175
"Black" (term), 28
"Black Americans" (term), 28
"Black" and "White" as racial descriptors, 168

Black communities and towns, 58–59
Blackdom, New Mexico, 59
Black Enterprise Magazine, 60
Black Entertainment Television (*BET*), 60
Black Lives Matter, 137–49
  and "guilty until proven innocent"
    assumption, 138–40
  names of those for whom we grieve,
    140–49
"Black-on-Black" crime, 64
"Black Wall Street," 58
Bland, Sandra, 143
bodies of Blacks, exploitation of, 40–41
Boley, Oklahoma, 59
bond decisions, 76
"bootstraps" rhetoric, 49–60
  absence of "bootstraps" (civil rights) of
    Black Americans, 50
  and Black communities/towns, 59
  and literacy barriers, 55–56
  relay team analogy for, 53–55
  and self-determination of Black people,
    60
  and Smalls's escape from enslavement,
    50–53
  and voter suppression, 56–58
Boyd, Rekia, 147
Bradford, Emantic "EJ" Fitzgerald, Jr.,
  141
Breckinridge, John, 132
Breckinridge Lane in Louisville,
  Kentucky, 132
Brisbon, Rumain, 144
Bronson, Po, 68–69
Brookings Institute, 46, 70
Brown, Carl, 60
Brown, Eddie, 60
Brown, Michael, Jr., 145, 193
Brown, Raheim, Jr., 148
Brown Capital Management, 60
Brown University, enslaved people's
  construction of, 45
The Butler (film), 198
Butler, Carrie, 71

Byrd, Robert, 156

Calhoun, Eben, 172–73
Cameron, Mary Benignus, 56
Campbell, Aaron, 149
Capitol building, U.S.
  enslaved people's construction of, 45
  insurrection of January 6, 2021, 19–20,
    21
Carey, Miriam Iris, 145
Carter, Chavis, 147
Castile, Philando, 139–40, 142, 193–94
Catholic Church and slavery, 89–90, 133
"Central Park Five" (1989), 77–78
Central Park incident (2020), 79, 80, 194
Chamberlain, Kenneth, Sr., 148
Chauvin, Derek, 41
Chicago Defender, 174
Christianity, 89–90, 91–92
Civil War, U.S., 51
Clark, Jamar O'Neal, 143
Clark, Stephon Alonzo, 142
Cleveland High School, Mississippi, 110
Clinton campaign (2008), 98
Cochran, McKenzie J., 145
Cohee, Kevin, 60
colleges and universities
  and consideration of race in admissions,
    120–21
  enslaved people's construction of, 45–
    46
  teaching inherent inferiority of Black
    people, 106–7
Colman, Mary Parkman (cousin), 179,
  182
colonists, European, 91
Columbine High School massacre (1999),
  64
comics, Black, 86
compassion, 16, 21
Confederate flags, 19
Contemporary Family Therapy, 134
Cooper, Amy, 79, 80, 194
Cooper, Christian, 79

corporations and unpaid labor of enslaved
Africans, 132–33
cotton industry, 46, 170–71
COVID-19, xi, 189, 190
Crawford, John, III, 145, 193
crime/crimes, 73–83
associating Black people with, 74
Black people falsely accused of, 74,
77–80
and "Central Park Five," 77–78
and criminal records, 117
and eugenics-related stereotypes, 106
gang-related, 65–66
hate crimes, 98
historical relationship to free labor, 74–
75, *160*
laws creating frivolous, 75
and rates of rearrest, 76–77
using race to label, 64–65
violent crime, 64–65, 77
See also law enforcement
criminal justice
and bond decisions, 76
desire for equality in, 42
and pretrial detention, 76–77
and sentencing practices, 81–82
See also crime/crimes; law
enforcement; prisons and imprisonment
Crutcher, Joey, xv, 191
Crutcher, Terence
author's grief for, xiv, 193
author's photo of, xiii, 193, 200
killed by law enforcement, xiii, 142,
192, 193
officer acquitted for murder of, xiii, xv
–xvi, 192, 194
protests following death of, xiii
Cuevas, Reynaldo, 147
Curls (beauty manufacturer), 60

"dangerous" neighborhoods, 62
Danner, Deborah, 142
"The Darker Your Skin, the More Likely
You'll End up in an American Jail"

(Merelli), 81
Davis, Shantel, 147
deaths of African Americans, 140–49
considered suspicious or dangerous, xii
police killings, xii, xiii, xv, 141–49,
192–94
in Spring 2020, xii
See also Arbery, Ahmaud; Crutcher,
Terence; Floyd, George Perry; Martin,
Trayvon; Taylor, Breonna
Declaration of Independence, 130
dehumanizing comments and jokes, 152–
53
Dellinger, Mahisha, 60
Denby, Gene, 115
difference, racial, 168–69
Dillard, Nehemiah Lazar, 147
discrimination, race-based, 36, 56–57
diversity, 5
*Diversity Explosion: How New Racial
Demographics are Remaking America*
(Frey), 69
domestic laborers, Black people expected
to be, 38–39, 173
Doubletree Hotel, Portland, Oregon, 79,
80
Doucet, Reginald, 148
Douglass, Margaret, 56
DuBose, Samuel Vincent, 143
Dum Diversas (papal bull), 89–90

East Chicago, Indiana, 178
Easton, Hosea, 93–94
East St. Louis Race Massacre, 109–10
economic benefits from slavery, 44–46
economic opportunities, absence of, 65,
66
education
barriers to, *159, 161*
and Black schools, *161*, 173
desire for equality in, 42, *163*
of Jessie Lee Mahone, 173–74
as opportunity associated with literacy,
56

pursuit of, *161*
and relay team analogy for inequality, 55
and teachers' perceptions of Black students, 80–81
See also colleges and universities; literacy and reading
Edwards, Jordan, 142
Edwards, Sharmel T., 147
elders in Black families, intentional amnesia among, 169–70
Ellis, C. P., 155–56
Ellis, Manuel "Mannie" Elijah, 141
Emory University, enslaved people's construction of, 45
equality
Black Americans' pursuit of, 39, 40, 44, *163*
in employment opportunities, 42, *163*
White resistance to, 109–10
See also inequality, race-based
eugenics, 106–8
"Even Babies Discriminate" (Bronson and Merryman), 68–69

familial bonds of African Americans, 126–28
family, American, 183
favors desired by Black people, 43–47
fear of Blacks experienced by Whites, 18, 184
Federal Housing Authority (FHA), 63
Ferrell, Jonathan, 145
Fifteenth Amendment to the Constitution, 56–57
Fisher, Abigail, 120
Flint, Michigan, 190
Florida, 56
Floyd, George Perry
author's grief for, xiv
killed by law enforcement, xii, xiii, 141, 193
and protests, 34, 153, 192
and undervaluation of Black bodies, 41

focus of Black people on race, 29–32
Fonville, Janisha, 144
Ford, Ezell, 144, 193
Fort Mose, Florida, 58
42 (film), 198
founding fathers, 130
Francis, Shereese, 147
fraternities, 126–27
Freedman's Village, Virginia, 59
free labor of Black people, 74–75, *160*.
See also slavery and enslaved people
Frey, Shelly Marie, 146
Frey, William H., 69
friendships with people of color, 70, 154
frustrations, cumulative, 39
FUBU (apparel manufacturer), 60
Fulton, Sybrina, *164*

Gaines, Korryn, 142
gangs, 65–66
Garner, Eric, 145, 193
Gary, Indiana
author's early life in, 2–3, 27
"dangerous" neighborhoods of, 62
high achievers from, 111–12
Parkman family photo, *186*
as safe environment, 62, 83
Whites' interaction with African Americans in, 6–7
Georgetown University, 46
Georgia, voter suppression in, 57, 58
gerrymandering, 57
Gilliam, Walter S., 80–81
Glenn, Brendon K., 143
Gospel Music Workshops of America, 191
government buildings built by enslaved people, 45
Graham, Ramarley, 148
Grant, Ulysses S., 130
Graves, Earl G., Jr., 60
Gray, Freddie Carlos, Jr., 143, 193
Gray, Kimani "Kiki," 146
"Great Migration" from the South, 169,

174, 177–78
Green, Jersey K., 147
Greenwood community in Tulsa,
  Oklahoma, 58–59
Griffin, Kitty (great-great grandmother),
  170, 174, 178, 182
groups of Black people, feeling rejected
  by, 125–28
guilt, feelings of, 154
"guilty until proven innocent"
  assumption, 75–76, 82–83, 138–40
guns, 79–80
Gurley, Akai Kareem, 144

Haley, Alex, 198
Hall, Mya Shawatza, 144
Hamilton, Dontre, 145, 193
happiness, opportunities to pursue, 39, 42
Harding, Kenneth, Jr., 148
Harris, Darnisha Diana, 146
Harris, Eric Courtney, 143, 193
Harris, Kamala, 19, 99, 102
Harrison, Ka Mauri, 79–80
Harrison, William Henry, 130
Harvard University, enslaved people's
  construction of, 45
hate crimes, 98
Hehir, Mary Thomasine, 56
The Help (film), 198
Henry, Danroy "DJ," Jr., 148
hierarchy, racial, 172–73
Hispanic people, 70
Hockaday, Meagan, 144
homelessness and vagrancy laws, 75
homeownership, barriers to, 63–64
hope, xiv, xvi
hopelessness, feelings of, 154
hotels, discriminatory practices of, 37
housing
  barriers to homeownership, 63–64
  and Black people stuck as perpetual
    tenants, 63, 66
  discriminatory practices in, 82
  and mortgages available to Whites, 63,

66
  pursuit of equality in, 42, 163
  and redlining practices, 63, 88
Howard, David, 33–34
"How Sexist, Racist Attacks on Kamala
  Harris Have Spread Online—A Case
  Study" (Tumulty, Woodsome, and
  Pecanha), 99
How to be an Antiracist (Kendi), 199
humor that dehumanizes others, 152–53
Hunter, Katherine Parkman (aunt), 178,
  186

ignorance of White Americans
  destructive nature of, 21
  education as remedy of, 21, 197, 198
  film and book recommendations, 198–
    99
  as fuel for fear, 18, 184
  origins of, 60
  and portrayals of Black people as
    dangerous, 197
  prevalence of, 17–18
  and unsupported negative stereotypes,
    111–12
immigrants, European
  basic opportunities enjoyed by, 55–56
  as "inner city" residents, 66
  and relay team analogy for inequality,
    54
I'm Still Here: Black Dignity in a World
  Made for Whiteness (Brown), 199
"incompetent" stereotype of Black
  people, 100
inequality, race-based
  Black people assumed to be domestic
    laborers, 38–39
  cumulative effects of, 46–47, 53–55
  discriminatory practices of hotels, 36–
    37
  and Jim Crow segregation, 36, 88, 134,
    162
  persistence of, 53
  relay team analogy for, 53–55

"inferiority" of Black people (debunked eugenics theory), 106–8
informed, staying, 152
"in-group preferences," 68–71
interracial relationships, 70–71, 177, 178

Jackson, Andrew, 130
Jackson, Larry Eugene, Jr., 146
January 6, 2021, insurrection at Capitol, 19–20
Jean, Botham Shem, 141
Jefferson, Atatiana Koquice, 141
Jefferson, Ervin Lee, III, 147
Jefferson, Thomas, 130
Jim Crow segregation, 36, 88, 134, *162*, 169
John, Daymond, 60
Johnson, Andrew, 130
Johnson, Robert L., 60
Johnson, Sheila, 60
Johnson administration, 121
jokes, dehumanizing, 152–53
Jones, Bettie "Betty Boo," 143
Jones, Corey Lamar, 143
Jones, Derrick, 148
JP Morgan Chase, 132–33
judgment of Black people, 30

Kager, India, 143
Kennedy, Randall, 93–94
Kennedy administration, 121
King, Billie Jean, 3
King, Martin Luther, Jr., 183
Kingman family, 50–51
Ku Klux Klan (KKK), 18

Laura, Dr. (talk radio personality), 86
law enforcement
  distrust of, 65
  and "guilty until proven innocent" assumption, 75–76, 138
  and lynchings, 173
  over-policing by, 41, 62, 65
  and police brutality, 65, 88

police killings of African Americans, xii, xiii, xv, 141–49, 192–94 (*see also* Crutcher, Terence; Floyd, George Perry; Taylor, Breonna)
  and pretrial detention, 76–77
  and rates of rearrest, 76–77
  skin color associated with likelihood of arrest by, 81
  and "War on Drugs" (1980s), 41–42
  See also prisons and imprisonment
"lazy" stereotype, 107
leadership, Black people in positions of, 99–100. See also Harris, Kamala; Obama, Barack
learning about people of color, 18, 154–55
lectures about racial differences, Black people invited to offer, 30–31
LeGrier, Quintonio, 143
Lehman Brothers, 132
Letter from a Birmingham Jail (King), 183
Levin, Josh, 114
literacy and reading
  barriers to, 55–56, *161*
  enslaved people barred from, 55–56, 93
  of Jessie Lee Mahone, 173–74
  opportunities associated with, 56
  and relay team analogy for inequality, 55–56
  of Smalls, 52
  and voter suppression, 57
Livingston, Kyam, 146
Loggins, Manual Levi, Jr., 148
Lopez, Andy, 145
Louisville, Kentucky
  and COVID-19 pandemic, xi
  tensions around Taylor's death, xii–xiii
Lyles, Charleena Chavon, 142
Lyles, fetus of Charleena Chavon, 142
lynchings, 88, 172–73, 177

Madison, James, 130
Mahone, Dennis (great-great

grandfather), 170, 174, 182
Mahone, Mary (aunt), 182, *186*
Mann, Joseph Curtis, 142
March on Washington (1963), *163*
Martin, Andy, 98
Martin, J. Alexander, 60
Martin, Tracy, *164*
Martin, Trayvon, xi–xii, xiv, 148, *164*, 193
Massey, Jermaine, 79
mass incarcerations, 36, 41–42, 88
McBride, Robin, 60
McBride-John, Andrea, 60
McBride Sisters Collection, 60
McCord, Charles H., 107–8
McCormick, Abigail Burnett, 59
McCray, Antron, 77
McDade, Kendrec, 147
McDole, Jeremy "Bam Bam," 143
McKee plantation in South Carolina, 50
McKenna, Natasha, 144
McVeigh, Timothy, 139
McWhorter, Frank, 59
Me and White Supremacy: Combat Racism, Change the World, and Become a Good Ancestor (Saad), 199
media
    anger of Black people portrayed in, 33
    Dr. Laura incident, 86
    inner-city crime associated with Black gangs, 65
    negative traits/outcomes emphasized by, 108–9
    one-sided coverage of Black communities, 62
    on protests, 34
Merelli, Annalisa, 81
Merrick, John, 60
Merryman, Ashley, 68–69
Michaelis, Arno, 156
middle class, Blacks blocked from, 64
migration of Black people to northern states, 169, 174, 177–78
Miller, Martha, 115

"Mississippi Appendectomies," 40, 41
Monk, Ellis, 81
Monroe, James, 130
Montgomery, Isaiah, 59
Moore, Aaron McDuffie, 60
Moore, Jamaal, Sr., 146
Moore, Kayla, 146
morality of Black people, attacks on, 107
mortgages, race-based accessibility of, 63, 66
Mound Bayou, Mississippi, 59
multiracial people, 70
Muslims, 90
My Life After Hate (Michaelis), 156

National Public Radio, 98, 115
National Rifle Association, xiii
Native American people, 183
nègre (French term), 89
negro (Spanish term), 89
"The Negro Christianized" (pamphlet), 91–92
neighborhoods, Black, 61–66
    barriers to homeownership in, 63–64
    crime and gangs in, 64–66
    long-term economic stagnation in, 63
    one-sided media coverage of events in, 62
    over-policing in, 62
    perpetual tenants in, 63
    and redlining practices, 63, 88
Neo-Nazis, 18
net worth of American families, average, 46
Nevarez, Gabriella Monique, 145
The New Jim Crow (Alexander), 41–42, 199
New Philadelphia, Illinois, 59
Newsweek, 68
New York Life, 132
Nicholas V, Pope, 89–90
Nicodemus, Kansas, 59
"niggardly" term employed by Howard, 33–34. *See also* "N" word

Norfolk Southern Railroad, 132
North Carolina Mutual Life Insurance
  Company, 60
"N" word, 85–95
  and author's marching band incident,
  11, 88–89
  and Dr. Laura controversy, 86
  entertainers' use of, 86
  etymology of, 89–92
  history of oppression association with,
  88, 94
  intention of injury embedded in, 93–94
  meaning derived from speaker, 87
  and "niggardly" term employed by
  Howard, 33–34
  in popular culture, 94–95
  and two-leg analogy, 87–88

Obama, Barack
  Byrd's endorsement of, 156
  challenges to citizenship, 98–99, 100,
  102
  election of, 97–103
  historic presidency of, 19
  success "tax" experienced by, 102
Oklahoma City bombing of (1995), 64,
  138–39
Okobi, Chinedu, 141
"OK" symbol of White power, 19
Olango, Alfred, 142
OneUnited Bank, 60
opportunities desired by Black people, 39
opposition, paradigm of, 168
outrage of Black people. See anger of
  Black people
"oversexualized" stereotype of Black
  people, 100–102

pagans, 90, 91
Palanco, Noel, 146
Parker, Dante, 144
Parkman, Jessie Lee Mahone (great-
  grandmother), 185, 186
  author's memories of, 179–80

birth of, 169–70
childhood of, 171
children of, 175–77
dark complexion of, 176–77, 180
death of, 181
descendants of, 186, 187
education of, 173–74
golden years of, 179–80
move to East Chicago, Indiana, 178, 183
relationship with John Walker Parkman,
  175–77, 179, 181
Parkman, John Henry (uncle), 176–77,
  178
Parkman, Johnnie Mae (grandmother),
  177, 178–79, 181, 182, 186
Parkman, John Walker (great-
  grandfather), 185
  death of, 179
  descendants of, 186, 187
  gravesite of, 183
  relationship with Jessie Lee, 175–77,
  179, 181
Parkman, Willie (uncle), 177, 178, 181,
  182–83, 186, 187
Pecanha, Sergio, 99
people of color (term), 28
Perrin, Keith, 60
Pew Research Center, 71
Pittsview, Alabama, 170, 172–73, 174,
  182
Planter steam ship, 51–52
polarization in America, 17
police. See law enforcement
political offices
  attacks on people holding, 99–100
  held by Smalls (former enslaved
  person), 52
Polk, James K., 130
poll taxes, 57
"Post-Traumatic Slave Syndrome"
  (PTSS), 135
poverty
  and barriers to basic opportunities, 159
  impact on Black communities, 62

and imprisonment, 116–17
    as portrayed in media, 109
    as related to work ethic, 115–16
    as self-perpetuating, 115–16
pre-formed opinions about African
    Americans, 6
present, staying intentionally, 153–54
presidential elections of 2016 and 2020,
    18–19
pretrial detention, 76–77
Price, Dante' Lamar, 148
prisons and imprisonment
    and criminal records, 117
    and free labor of Black people, 74–75,
    160
    and mass incarcerations, 36, 41–42, 88
    of people in poverty, 116–17
    unequal sentences received by Black
    people in, 42
privilege of White Americans
    and attempts at interacting with Black
    groups, 128
    basic opportunities enjoyed by, 55
    and "bootstraps" paradigm, 50
    and economic benefits from slavery,
    45–46
    as tool for addressing injustices, 152
protests attended and led by Black
    people, 34, 153, 192
Proud Boys, 18
Provident Hospital, Chicago, Illinois,
    60
Prudence Crossing, Alabama, 170–71,
    174, 182–83
public assistance, 113–17
    as necessity, 117
    as related to work ethic, 115–16
    stigmatization of, 115
    and "Welfare Queen" stereotype, 114–
    15
Pullman Porters, 174

race
    concept of, 90–91
    as dominant concern of Black people,
    29–32
    perceived as most salient characteristic
    about people of color, 31
    questions about, xx
    racial bias, becoming sensitized to, 152–
    53
    racial injustice, responding to, 151–56
    racial tension and unrest
        and author's message to School of
        Music, xiii–xiv, xvi, 188–200
        in Louisville, Kentucky, xii
        and "Safe Saturday Conversations
        about Race," xvi–xvii
        in Spring 2020, xi–xiii, 189
        White Americans' responses to, 17, 196
racist (definition), xix–xx, 155
Ramos, Michael Brent Charles, 141
rape of Black women, 41, 175–76
rappers, Black, 86
Reagan, Ronald, 114, 115
redefining/repurposing, African
    American culture's embrace of, 87–88
redlining practices, 36, 63, 88
"Red Summer" (1921), 177
Reed, Dreasjon "Sean," 141
Reid, Jerame C., 144
relay team analogy for inequality, 53–55
reminders of race and racial differences,
    30–31
"Residual Effects of Slavery: What
    Clinicians Need to Know," 134–35
resilience of Black Americans, 58
Reuters, 98
REWIRE program to unlearn racism, 155
Rice, Tamir, 144, 193
Richardson, Kevin, 77
Roberts, Elijah, 59
Roberts, Hansel, 59
Robertson, Chad, 142
Roberts Settlement, Hamilton County,
    Indiana, 59
Robinson, Tamon, 147
Robinson, Tony Terrell, Jr., 144, 193

Roediger, David, 90–91
Romper Room (television show), 3–4
Roots (miniseries), 198
Rose, Antwon, Jr., 141
Rosewood, Florida, 58
Roundtree, Charles "Chop," Jr., 141
Russell, Timothy, 146

"Safe Saturday Conversations about Race," xvi–xvii
Salaam, Yusef, 77
Sandy Hook School shooting (2012), 64
Santana, Raymond, 77
Schlessinger, Laura, 86
schools, Black, *161*. See also education
Scott, Walter Lamar, 143, 193
segregation era, 36, 88, 134, *162*
self-determination of Black people, 59
Selma (film), 198
Seneca Village, New York City, 58
sentencing practices, 81–82
sexual stereotypes of Black people, 100–102
sharecropping communities, 170–71
Shelby, Betty, xiii, xv–xvi, 192
Shelby, Isaac, 132
Shelbyville Road in Louisville, Kentucky, 132
Shelton, Lee (father), *186*
Shelton, Terralyn (Roach; sister), *186*
Shelton, Tobi Lorraine Upshaw (mother), 178–79, *186*
Shepherd, Jasmine, 110
shopping, discrimination experienced while, 82–83
"6MWE" references, 19–20
skin, Black
  and African people perceived as inferior, 91–92
  negative associations with, 89, 93
slavery and enslaved people, 36, 52
  abolition of, 74–75, 130
  and African people perceived as inferior, 91–92
  and ancestry of African Americans, 131
  caring for White children, *158*
  and Catholic Church, 89–90, 133
  contemporary reminders of, 131–32
  as cornerstone of American economy, 44
  and cumulative effects of inequality, 46–47
  economic benefits from, 44–46
  and economic blow of abolition, 74
  erasure of personal identities, 131
  and exploitation of Black bodies, 40–41
  families fragmented by, 41, 93, 131, 171
  forced "breeding" of women in, 41, 92
  and founding fathers, 130
  intergenerational trauma from, 134–35
  letting go of the past and moving on from, 129–35
  and literacy, 55–56, 93
  long-term impacts of, 46–47
  and marital relationships, 50–51, 92–93, 171
  and privilege of modern White Americans, 45
  and property ownership, 93
  and rape of women, 41, 92
  and relay team analogy for inequality, 54–55
  and Residual Effects of Slavery, 134–35
  slave ship diagram, *157*
  Smalls's successful escape from, 50–53
  and surnames of African Americans, 130–31
  unpaid debt of, 133–34
  and wealth gap, 46–47, 133
Smalls, Hannah, 50–51
Smalls, Robert, 50
Smith, Susan, 78, 80
Smith, Yvette, 145
social circles, preference for White, 67–71
sororities, 126–27

The Souls of Black Folk (DuBois), 198
South
and birth/death certificates of Black
people, 175
and economic blow of abolition, 74
free labor of "criminal" Black people
in, 74–75, *160*
interracial relationships in, 70–71, 177,
178
Jim Crow segregation in, 36, 88, 134,
162, 169
lynchings in, 88, 172–73, 177
migration of Black people to northern
states, 169, 174, 177–78
"Red Summer" (1921), 177
voter suppression in, 57
South Carolina House of Representatives,
52
So You Want to Talk About Race (Oluo),
199
Spaulding, C. C., 60
special favors desired by Black people,
43–47
Spring 2020, xi, xii
Stanley-Jones, Aiyana Mo'Nay, 149
Starbucks, Black men arrested at, 78, 80
stereotypes
and feeling threatened by successful
Black people, 106
leaders attacked with, 99–100
sexual stereotypes, 100–102
unsupported negative, 110–12
sterilization, forced, 40, 41
Sterling, Alton, 143
Sterling, Terrence LeDell, 142
successful Black people, feeling
threatened by, 105–12
and eugenics' influence, 106–8
ignorance contributing to, 111–12
and media's portray of Black people,
108–9
and pervasive negative stereotypes, 106
and racially motivated violence, 109–10
and Shepherd's valedictorian status,

110
success "tax" experienced people of
color, 102
Sullivan, Mary Scholastica, 56
surnames of African Americans, 130–31
"suspicious" African Americans, xii, xiv,
82–83
symbols of racism, 19–20
syphilis experiments conducted by U.S.
Public Health Service, 40
systemic racism, 39–40

talks about racial differences, Black
people invited to offer, 30–31
Taylor, Breonna
author's grief for, xiv
killed by law enforcement, xii, 141, 193
protests following death of, xii–xiii, 34,
153, 192
Taylor, Linda, 114–15
Taylor, Zachary, 130
teachers' perceptions of Black students,
80–81
terminology, racial, 28
terrorism against Black people, 36, 57,
173
textiles, 45
Thirteenth Amendment of the U.S.
Constitution, 36, 74–75, 130, 133
Thomas, Alesia, 147
threat, people of color perceived as, 18,
193
Thurmond, Strom, 70–71
tragedies, racial, 153–54, 195–96
trauma
following racial tragedies, 153–54,
195–96
intergenerational, 134–35
*A Treatise on the Intellectual Character
and Civil and Political Condition of the
Colored People of the United States: and
the Prejudice Exercised Towards Them*
(Easton), 93–94
Trump, Donald

and "Birtherism," 99
and Capitol insurrection, 19
and "Central Park Five," 77–78, 80
and White supremacist groups, 18–19
Tulsa, Oklahoma
   All Souls Unitarian Church in, 155
   Greenwood community in, 58–59
   housing discrimination in, 82
   race massacre in (1921), 38
   racial prejudice toward author in, 38–39
   and Shelby's acquittal for Crutcher's
      murder, xiii, xv–xvi, 192, 194
   See also Crutcher, Terence
Tumulty, Karen, 99
"The Tuskegee Experiment," 40, 41
Twelve Years a Slave (film), 198
Tyler, John, 130

unemployment and vagrancy laws, 75,
   170
United States Public Health Service, 40
University of Louisville
   author's message to School of Music,
      xiii–xiv, xvi, 188–200
   and COVID-19 pandemic, xi
   response to Taylor's death, xiii–xiv
University of North Carolina, enslaved
   people's construction of, 45
University of Tulsa, 38
Unlimited Praise Gospel Choir, 191
U.S. House of Representatives, 52

vagrancy laws, 75, 160, 170
Valparaiso University
   author's arrival at, 3–5
   author's experiences with racism at,
      10–12
   author's experience with stereotyping
      at, 100–102
   author's graduation from, 12–14
   author's heightened alertness in, 37–38
   author's invisibility at, 12–14
   author's marching band incident, 11,
      88–89

Black population at, 5
   Crusader mascot of, 10
   culture shock of, 5–6, 7
   navigating Whiteness at, 5–6, 16
   reminders of racial differences at, 30
Van Buren, Martin, 130
Vassell, Saheed, 141
violence
   and historical scholarship on West
      Africans, 108
   lynchings, 88, 172–73, 177
   racially motivated, 58, 109–10
   "Red Summer" (1921), 177
   using race to label, 64
   violent crime, 64–65, 77
Virginia Criminal Code, 56
voting rights
   pursuit of equality in, 163
   and voter suppression, 36, 56–58, 88,
      159

Wachovia Corporation, 132
wages, 56
Walden, Micajah, 59
"War on Drugs" (1980s), 41–42
Warren, Johnnie Kamahi, 146
Washington, George, 130
Washington, Steven Eugene, 149
Washington & Lee University, enslaved
   people's construction of, 45
Washington Post, 79–80, 99
Washington-Williams, Essie Mae, 71
wealth and financial security
   and barriers to homeownership, 64–65
   and barriers to middle class, 65
   intergenerational transfer of, 46–47, 56
   wealth gap in America, 46–47, 133
   See also poverty
"Welfare Queen" stereotype, 114–15. See
   also public assistance
West Africans, biased observations about,
   107–8
West Side Story (1961 musical), 65
When They See Us (film), 78

White, Phillip Gregory, 144, 193
White, Victor, III, 145
White House, enslaved people's
   construction of, 45
Whiteness and Whites, 5–6
   addressing racial injustice, 151–56
   as audience of book, 27
   author's college experiences with, 3–7
   author's early experiences with, 2–3
   fear experienced by, 18, 184
   good intentions of majority, 20
   impending minority status of, 69–70
   intergenerational transfer of wealth, 46–
   47
   mortgages available to, 63, 66
   opposition to affirmative action, 120,
   122, 168
   and police killing of Crutcher, xv
   in positions of authority, 7
   and preference for White social circles,
   67–71
   pre-formed opinions about African
   Americans, 6
   privilege of, 45–46, 50, 55, 128, 152
   resistance to racial equality, 109–10
   and "Safe Saturdays," xvii
   struggles with race and racism, 20–21
   terms, 28
   See also ignorance of White Americans
White supremacist groups and beliefs,
   18–19, 133, 155
Wilberforce University, 60
Williams, Anthony, 33
Williams, Barrington "BJ," 145
Williams, Daniel Hale, 60
Williams, Derek, 148
Williams, Malissa, 146
Wise, Korey, 77
Woodsome, Kate, 99
work ethic, 115–16
Wright, Daunte, 141

Yale University, 45

Zimmerman, George, xii, *164*

For more information, contact:
garyspringsip@gmail.com

Made in the USA
Middletown, DE
21 October 2022